MARGOT STEELE

BEGINNER'S GUIDE TO CHAKRAS

Unlock Your Inner Energy and
Achieve Balance
(2024 Novice Crash Coursed)

Copyright © 2024 by Margot Steele

All rights reserved. No part of this publication may be reproduced, stored or transmitted in any form or by any means, electronic, mechanical, photocopying, recording, scanning, or otherwise without written permission from the publisher. It is illegal to copy this book, post it to a website, or distribute it by any other means without permission.

First edition

This book was professionally typeset on Reedsy. Find out more at reedsy.com

Contents

1	An Overview of the Chakras	1
2	The Chakras' Past	13
3	The Chakra of the Root	14
4	The Chakra of Sacral	22
5	Chakra of the Solar Plexus	33
6	Chakra of the Heart	44
7	Grasping Chakra	56
8	Chakra of the Third Eye	67
9	The Crown Chakra	86
10	In summary	95

1

An Overview of the Chakras

Let us explain what a chakra is to you first. The Sanskrit word "chakra" can be understood to refer to the energy wheel. We are surrounded by energy, which vibrates at various frequencies. The universe is full with energy, even in dimensions that are ordinarily invisible to us—the spiritual realms, for example. Life force energy, which permeates everything that exists or has ever existed, is abundant throughout the universe. It circulates throughout the body and is constantly in contact with us.

Chakras: What Are They?

A chakra is a gathering point for energy within the body that enables optimal functioning and health. There are seven primary chakras and numerous minor ones. This book focuses on the major chakras because they have the greatest impact on healing and well-being.

When chakras experience blockages, proper energy flow and distribution throughout the body are disrupted, leading to various illnesses and poor health. This unhealthy state affects the physical, mental/emotional, and spiritual aspects of a person. Therefore, healing the chakras can significantly impact overall health.

Chakras can also become unbalanced, resulting in overactivity of certain parts of ourselves and leading to dysfunctional behavior or ill health. Each chakra vibrates at a unique energetic frequency, similar to light.Consequently, chakras are associated with different colors, ranging from lower to higher energy, which coincides with the colors of the rainbow.

Additionally, each chakra is associated with an element and a specific location in the body. Chakras are not energy themselves but rather areas where energy congregates.In a healthy individual, energy flows freely and interacts with the body, mind, soul, and the universe, leading to a harmonious balance. When all chakras are open and balanced, one can experience a sense of harmony, peace, and contentment.

Base Chakra

AN OVERVIEW OF THE CHAKRAS

Of all the chakras, the root chakra is the most basic. It gives you a basic sense of grounding by "rooting" you in Mother Earth. It has to do with feeling safe and secure as well as having the means to meet your fundamental requirements, which include food, drink, and shelter. The root chakra and a sense of safety and security are strongly related. The root chakra is situated at the base of the spine, and red is its related hue. This is a reflection of the root chakra's lower vibrational frequency compared to the other seven major chakras.

Chakra Sacral

The sacral chakra is located directly above the root chakra. It is linked to your creativity, sexuality, and capacity for enjoyment. Because it affects higher functions of your being than the root chakra, it has a greater vibrational frequency. If they have not satisfied the most basic requirements for their security, such as having access to food and water, the majority of individuals will not be experiencing joy and creativity. Right below the navel is where you'll find the sacral chakra.

Chakra of the Solar Plexus

The solar plexus chakra is linked to the ego's higher order functioning. This involves accepting responsibility, having a sense of purpose in your work, and having self-confidence. Having open and balanced root, sacral, and solar plexus chakras allows you to take charge of your life and behave with self-control and confidence. Yellow is the hue connected to the solar plexus chakra. It is situated behind the rib cage and directly above the navel.

Heart Chakra

The heart chakra is linked to acceptance, tolerance, love, and empathy. This transcends romantic love, even though the heart chakra is unquestionably connected to romantic love. The heart chakra is the source of all forms of love, including self-acceptance and love for oneself. Although pink-colored stones and crystals are also effective in treating the heart chakra, the heart chakra is green in color. The middle of the chest is where the heart chakra is situated.

Grasping Chakra

Situated in the lower throat region, the throat chakra is the first spiritual chakra. The position of the throat chakra suggests that it has to do with telling the truth and communicating. The throat chakra has a blue hue.

Third Eye Chakra

The third eye chakra is situated above the actual eyes in the middle of the brow. It is also connected to the pineal gland, a tiny organ found in the brain. Since ancient times, the third eye has been understood to be our window into the psychic and intuitive domains. As a result, this is a "eye" that gathers data from non-physical realms. All of us possess intuitive abilities, but we are unable to use them if the third eye is closed. Thankfully, your third eye chakra may be opened and healed. This chakra is incredibly energizing. Indigo is the hue connected to the third eye chakra.

The Crown Chakra

The top of the head is where the crown chakra is situated, while some experts say it is somewhat above the top of the head. It has a close relationship to the nerve system and brain. The crown chakra is linked to consciousness and awareness as its primary function. But because the crown chakra opens our channels to our spirituality and Higher Self, it goes much beyond this. It is linked to happiness, presence, and wisdom. The crown chakra is fundamentally linked to spiritual oneness within the world and communication with higher planes of consciousness. The crown chakra's primary hue is purple, although it's also connected to white and gold.

How Do Chakras Resolve?

"In the upcoming pages, we will discuss the indicators of a blocked or imbalanced chakra. If you find that you are experiencing blocked chakras, rest assured that you are not alone. In contemporary Western society, particularly in the modern world, a majority of individuals lead unhealthy and unbalanced lives. It is highly likely that most people have imbalanced chakras.Regrettably, due to our increasingly materialistic and atheistic beliefs, numerous individuals are not even aware of this fact or willing to consider the possibility that they require more than physical healing. There are several methods available to heal, balance, and awaken your chakras. One of the primary techniques is daily meditation.We will delve into various ways to meditate for just a few minutes each day, which can significantly contribute to chakra healing. Additionally, chakras can also be restored through yoga, daily affirmations, and the skillful use of colors. The use of crystals is another popular practice, as they possess specific vibrations that can store and transmit spiritual energy. These vibrations align with the spiritual essence of each chakra, reflecting their individual meanings. The following sections will introduce the seven major chakras, with each receiving its own dedicated chapter in this book."

Equilibrium Chakra Systems

In the following chapters, we will delve into the specific symptoms of blocked chakras and the procedures for healing and unblocking each of the seven main chakras.In this section, we will provide an overview of the general procedures used for chakra healing.

If you are new to this concept, there may be a tendency to focus on the spiritual chakras right away. However, it is likely that you have some level of blockages in your lower chakras. To maintain the appropriate balance, it is crucial to address and heal the lower chakras before moving on to the higher-level ones. For instance, if your root chakra is blocked and you are struggling with essential aspects of your life, negative energies will impact and block your higher-level chakras as well. It would be challenging to devote energy to unconditional love, truthfulness, and psychic abilities when you are constantly feeling unsafe and anxious due to a blocked root chakra. Although some individuals may be able to manage this, the reality is that most people would not succeed.

Think of this process as building a house. You first construct the foundation, and if it is not done correctly, the rest of the house becomes unstable and unsafe.Remember that your spiritual journey is lifelong, so be patient as you work towards your goals. Those who are patient will reap greater rewards.

There are seven methods you can utilize to heal and balance your chakras, thereby promoting optimal physical, mental, emotional, and spiritual well-being. We will briefly outline each of these below.

Meditation

There are several benefits of meditation. Meditation is a mind-freeing and nerve-calming practice. You can work with each of the chakras using visualization techniques during meditation. The specifics and fundamental techniques of meditation will be covered in the upcoming chapters.

Yoga

Although doing yoga is not necessary, it can be a very useful tool for those who do. You may encourage natural energy flow by physically opening your chakras with the use of yoga. It also offers numerous health advantages for the body, including balancing and healing your chakras and enhancing flexibility and tone.

Breathing

Breathing exercises can be performed independently or in conjunction with meditation and yoga to calm the nerves and increase energy flow in the body.

Vocalization and Sound

Various methods can be used to associate sounds with healing the chakras, such as using single tones, mantras, or daily affirmations to reprogram the subconscious mind and achieve goals. Additionally, music can support these efforts.

Colors

Each of the seven major chakras is linked to a specific color that reflects its vibrational energy level. To work on a particular chakra, surrounding oneself with its associated colors can be done through clothing, crystals, and even using those colors in the home or meditation space.

Food

Selecting the right foods is crucial for chakra healing, and utilizing color as a guide can be helpful. The coloration of a food item corresponds to its energy level.For instance, to balance the root chakra, increasing the consumption of red-colored foods is advisable.

Essential Oils

Essential oils can also contribute to chakra healing as each oil vibrates at a specific energetic frequency. Applying essential oils to the skin or inhaling their scents can be beneficial. In the following chapter, we will focus on the root chakra, starting at the lowest point. A thorough exploration of the root chakra will be provided, including a discussion on blockage symptoms for readers to identify if their root chakra is blocked.

2

The Chakras' Past

The concept of the chakras, which are energy centers in the body, was introduced to the Western culture over 100 years ago. However, the origin of these ideas can be traced back much further. Initially, the chakras emerged in Tantrik traditions as centers where energy gathered before flowing throughout the body, rather than being the sources of energy themselves. Originally, these energy centers were not perceived as tangible entities but were based on empirical observations. Through these observations, it was noticed that emotions and sensations were experienced in specific areas of the body, connecting the physical aspects with the mental, emotional, and spiritual states that humans commonly encounter. Therefore, while these ideas were symbolic and conceptual, they were grounded in real, observable, and physical experiences. Subsequently, between 1500 and 500 BC, these ideas evolved and were recorded in ancient Indian texts known as the Vedas. It was during this time that they became associated with the notion of spinning wheels of energy and light. Over the course of more than a thousand years, these concepts were studied and refined until they were formalized in the 1600s by an influential Indian guru named Swami Purandanda. In the early 20th century, Swami Purandanda's ideas were translated into English, gradually gaining popularity and acceptance across various parts of the Western world. The knowledge of the chakras and the practice of yoga became widespread after the 1960s.

3

The Chakra of the Root

Of the seven primary chakras, the root chakra is the lowest and most basic. It is situated at the spine's base. Four lotus leaves are used to symbolically depict the red color of the root chakra. The root chakra is called Muladhara in Sanskrit.

The Root Chakra: What Is It?

The base of the spine is where the root chakra is located, and it extends up the lowest three vertebrae. The primary function of the root chakra is to provide a feeling of safety and security. "Anhara" is a Sanskrit term that translates to "support," so the word Muladhara can be translated as "root support." The root chakra is categorized as a matter chakra because it is associated with physical well-being. It signifies that you have a firm footing on the ground, feel secure, and are capable of meeting your basic needs. These essential needs include safety, food, water, and shelter for everyone. With money being crucial in meeting these needs in today's world, the root chakra is also linked to basic financial security. However, this does not imply that it is connected to becoming wealthy or earning a high income. It simply means earning enough money to fulfill your basic needs and maintain financial stability. Building upon the analogy of a house, the root chakra is comparable to its foundation. Just as you wouldn't rush the construction of a house if you plan to reside in it for a long time, it is essential to establish a solid foundation to ensure stability in your life. In order to fully open any of the higher chakras, the needs related to the root chakra must be fulfilled. Even if you don't exhibit symptoms of a blocked root chakra, it is advisable for beginners in the study of chakras, meditation, and yoga to focus on the root chakra to ensure its well-being and complete openness. It is highly probable that as a beginner, your chakras are not properly open and balanced. Therefore, it is crucial to be patient and take the necessary time to work on your chakras. Gaining the proper understanding and skills will benefit you in the future. Moreover, the root chakra is associated with various basic emotions, which can include unhealthy ones. If you are experiencing anxiety, fear, or doubt, it could be an indication of a blocked root chakra. Trust is closely linked to the root chakra, as well as other chakras. A lack of trust in others often stems from fear, and a sense of anxiety can arise from feeling unsafe and lacking control over your own life. Having a balanced root chakra involves feeling that you are ultimately in control of your life.

How a Block Affects the Root Chakra

The root chakra can be obstructed by various experiences, but one's childhood experiences have a significant influence on it. When you are a young child, you are highly attuned to the feeling of safety.If you had caring and stable parents who provided a secure home environment, you would have felt completely safe as a child. This sense of safety may persist into adulthood, but there are events throughout life that can disrupt the root chakra. One way the root chakra can be blocked is through inconsistent care during childhood.When a child's needs are met sporadically and unpredictably, it can lead to a blocked root chakra. Any form of abuse experienced during childhood will certainly result in a blockage of the root chakra. Inconsistent treatment during childhood can also hinder the root chakra. A caregiver with unpredictable mood swings can have a detrimental impact as the child never knows when the parent will become angry, causing feelings of fear and insecurity.

Any negative experience that significantly affects one's ability to feel safe or trust others can also block the root chakra.Sexual assault and rape are major reasons why many individuals, especially women, have a blocked root chakra.This is one way the root chakra can become blocked in adulthood. Another event that can lead to a blocked chakra at any time is a home invasion.Even if a person was not present during the break-in, it can leave them feeling unsafe and violated.

Signs of a Root Chakra Blockage

There are numerous signs indicating a blocked root chakra, many of which are connected to a general sense of anxiety. If one feels unsafe, it is a clear indication of a blockage in their root chakra.This feeling of unsafety can manifest in various forms, such as feeling unsafe at home. Many individuals who feel unsafe at home desire to relocate to a better place but are unable to do so due to financial constraints. This is a definite symptom of a blocked root chakra since it involves both a feeling of unsafety and an inability to meet financial needs. Being financially insecure is another indicator of a blocked root chakra.This can manifest as constantly struggling to pay bills and accumulating significant debt that interferes with fulfilling basic needs. Additionally, it can present as financial instability, such as irregular income.If one faces challenges in managing their finances, it is advisable to suspect a blocked root chakra. Anxiety disorders, a persistent sense of fear and uncertainty, and nightmares are common symptoms of a blocked root chakra.These symptoms may or may not be accompanied by restlessness. Restlessness often arises from a lack of foundational grounding in one's life.It is coupled with a general sense of insecurity as there is a conscious or subconscious awareness of the inability to meet basic needs. Many individuals develop a blocked root chakra due to inconsistent treatment or abandonment during childhood, resulting in a vague feeling of being abandoned as adults. If one experiences feelings of abandonment, it strongly indicates the need to work on healing the root chakra. Failing to meet financial needs can lead to co-dependency and relying on others, such as friends or relatives, to continually bail one out of financial issues or lend money regularly to make ends meet. While borrowing small amounts of money occasionally may not be a significant symptom, continuously relying on borrowing money indicates a blocked root chakra. Depending on others to fulfill basic needs or struggling to meet them securely can result in feelings of guilt and resentment. It can also lead to depression and a sense of helplessness.A blocked chakra affects every aspect of one's being. If the root chakra is blocked, it is so fundamental that it may hinder the individual from experiencing anything related to other chakras. This can cause a lack of self-confidence and an inability to fully experience sexuality, pleasure, and express creativity. In severe cases, spirituality may also be out of reach. Additionally, many individuals with a blocked root chakra may experience physical symptoms. These physical symptoms commonly affect the lower parts of the body, such as experiencing sciatica or chronic foot and leg pain. Digestive issues like regular bouts of diarrhea and constipation can occur.Men may face prostate problems, while women may experience urinary tract infections and menstruation issues.

Recipes for Root Chakra Healing

You can dedicate some time to consuming foods that are especially beneficial for opening up the root chakra. Think about root vegetables first. They contain vibrations of basic energy that, when they grow in the earth, can assist repair your root chakra. These consist of garlic, onions, radishes, potatoes, and carrots. Another option is to concentrate on eating foods that are red in hue. Consuming tomatoes is a great way to nourish your root chakra. In addition to being a root vegetable, beets are a great option because of their reddish hue. Pumpkin seeds and sweet potatoes are also beneficial.

Essential Oils for Chakra Root

Consider utilizing relaxing essential oils to aid in the healing of the root chakra. Sandalwood is a fantastic example of an essential oil for the root chakra. With the use of this essential oil, you may help to relax your nervous system and free yourself from the bad energy that is connected to worry and fear. Working with the root chakra is another beneficial use for myrrh essential oil. Additionally, it calms and soothes the neurological system.

The Root Chakra's Colors

Colors can be utilized to aid in the healing of the root chakra. The primary color recommended for healing this chakra is red.There are various activities that can be carried out during the healing process in order to incorporate colors.One option is to wear clothing that is colored red. This practice can be implemented at any given time, but it is particularly beneficial during yoga sessions or meditation. Another approach involves adorning one's living space with red-colored items, such as pillows, sheets, throws, and drapes. The objective is to constantly immerse oneself in the energy associated with the root chakra, which is strongly linked to the color red.Additionally, placing red flowers around the home or office can be beneficial, as well as hanging paintings that prominently feature the color red. For individuals seeking healing of the root chakra, surrounding oneself with as much red energy as possible can be highly advantageous.

Crystals for Chakra Root

Crystals can have a significant role in the healing process of your chakras. To gain a deeper understanding, please refer to my book on Crystal Healing. When it comes to the root chakra, it is recommended to utilize crystals that are red or black in color. The key factor in their effectiveness is the energy they possess, rather than their specific hue. There are four highly recommended crystals for this purpose: garnet, hematite, black tourmaline, and obsidian. Another excellent choice is ruby. If you feel insecure in your living space, it is advisable to place four black tourmaline stones in the corners of the room. Crystals can also be placed in your car or worn as accessories to aid in the healing of the root chakra, reduce anxiety, and enhance your overall sense of safety. Holding hematite in your hands, whether for relaxation or during meditation, is believed to have a grounding and reassuring effect.

Root Chakra Meditation

Healing the chakras can be achieved through the practice of meditation, which is considered the most crucial tool. While there are various types of meditation, this beginner's book recommends focusing on the conventional method. This method entails visualizing a spinning energy wheel that matches the color of the respective chakra. Before starting meditation, it is essential to decide where, when, and for how long you will meditate. It is advised to meditate once or twice a day, with each session lasting at least 15 minutes. If time allows, a 30-minute meditation is also acceptable. It is normal to encounter difficulties in meditation initially, especially if you are new to it, as it takes time to train the mind to concentrate and eliminate thoughts. Achieving a clear mind is a vital aspect of meditation, considering that people typically have busy minds constantly filled with thoughts, concerns, and internal dialogues. This is particularly true for individuals with blocked root chakras, which can lead to an overactive mind consumed by worries about financial issues or the desire for change. The objective of meditation is to achieve complete mental calmness, free from any inner voices or thoughts. Your chosen meditation space should be comfortable, quiet, and free from distractions if you live with others or have children. Optionally, soft Indian, Chinese, or Japanese music can be played during meditation, or silence can be preferred. The meditation pose recommended is called the easy pose, also known as Sukhasana in Sanskrit, which involves sitting on the floor with crossed legs. If sitting on the floor becomes uncomfortable, using a pillow for support is recommended. Beginners may also find it helpful to lean against a wall or some other object for back support.

To initiate the meditation process, close your eyes and take slow, deep breaths.Take a few moments to focus solely on your breath, letting go of any thoughts. To aid in clearing your mind, direct your attention to your breath.Breathe naturally or, if it relaxes you, breathe in through your nose and exhale through your mouth.

Now, imagine a completely black space to visualize.Envision the darkest black possible, a deep, inky blackness. Next, visualize a distant red light. Slowly picture this red light as either a slowly rotating disk or a spinning lotus flower with four petals, as shown in the illustration at the start of this chapter.

Watch as the red light gradually grows larger as it approaches you. Imagine it entering your body and ascending slowly to the base of your spine where the root chakra resides. As it nears, observe it expanding in size. Once it enters your root chakra, visualize it spinning faster. With each inhalation, envision the disk of light or flower growing in size; as you exhale, see it shrink. Maintain this practice until you have completed your designated meditation time.

Another technique you can incorporate during meditation is to recite the mantra "LAM" to generate the appropriate energy level.

Positive Thoughts for the Root Chakra

Affirmations serve as self-statements that aid in training our subconscious mind. The presence of blockages in a chakra often arises from beliefs residing in the subconscious, which were imprinted by caregivers and past experiences. These belief systems may govern our lives without our complete awareness. Therefore, engaging in daily affirmations can effectively reverse these ingrained thought patterns.

Here are several examples of affirmations that can assist in healing the root chakra:
- I am secure.
- I am shielded.
- I am capable of meeting my own needs.
- Mother Earth will provide for my well-being and offer protection.
- My home is a safe haven.
- I experience a sense of safety and stability.

While repeating these affirmations, you may further amplify the energy by holding a crystal in your hand. It is advisable to say these affirmations as frequently as required, at a minimum of once per day. Uttering them before going to sleep ensures their penetration into the subconscious mind.

4

The Chakra of Sacral

This chapter focuses on the second chakra, known as the sacral chakra. The healing and opening of the sacral chakra depend on the healing and opening of the root chakra. Maintaining a balanced state among all the chakras is crucial, as an imbalance or blockage can lead to various difficulties in life. Therefore, it is important to not only concentrate on healing the chakras but also avoid excessive focus on any one chakra. The sacral chakra is represented by the color orange and symbolized by six lotus petals. Its Sanskrit name is Svadhishthana. Similar to the root chakra, the sacral chakra is associated with the material aspects of life.

Chakra Sacral: What Is It?

The sacral chakra is connected to sexuality, the capacity to feel pleasure, and creativity.It is also associated with reproductive functions and intense emotions. Due to its link with sexuality and reproduction, the sacral chakra plays a significant role in relationships, sensuality, and the associated emotions. Fantasies, including sexual fantasies, as well as any form of creative imagination, are also linked to an open and balanced sacral chakra.

Maintaining balance is crucial for the sacral chakra, as observed in how people live their lives and the challenges they face. An open yet unbalanced sacral chakra can lead to addictive behaviors, particularly sexual addiction. This excessive focus on seeking sexual partners and engaging in sexual activities can have detrimental effects on other aspects of their lives due to the lack of equilibrium. The key to a balanced sacral chakra lies in being able to enjoy various pleasures without being overwhelmed by them.

An imbalanced sacral chakra, associated not only with sexuality but also with sensuality and experiencing different pleasures, can manifest in various ways. For instance, individuals with this imbalance may develop a gambling addiction, becoming obsessed and experiencing difficulties in managing their finances.Another manifestation of an unbalanced sacral chakra is an excessive devotion to fantasies. While it is normal to fantasize to some extent, when these fantasies dominate and interfere with real life, they become destructive.This can include excessive sexual fantasies that hinder real sexual relationships or nonsexual dreams that never materialize.

People with an out-of-balance sacral chakra who are big dreamers tend to constantly envision different possibilities but fail to take any practical steps to achieve them. Drug and alcohol addiction can also stem from an imbalanced sacral chakra, either partly or entirely. Blocked sacral chakras can prevent individuals from experiencing pleasure, leading them to constantly seek it out without ever truly attaining it or having a high threshold for even the slightest sensations of pleasure. This can result in risky behaviors, substance abuse, and other addictions. Furthermore, extreme athletes often exhibit a blocked sacral chakra as they engage in increasingly dangerous activities to obtain even the slightest hint of enjoyment.

When you study the different chakras, you will understand how problems in one chakra can be related to difficulties in other chakras. Such problems rarely occur in isolation because individuals with blocked chakras generally have overall health and soul issues. If you were on a solid spiritual path, learning about the chakras, prana, and kundalini energy, as well as regularly practicing yoga and meditation, your problems would be minimized. As you study the chakras, it is beneficial to examine each chakra and consider how they can connect in terms of the emotions and behaviors that manifest in your life. We have already provided an example of how sacral chakra problems can cause financial issues due to root chakra problems in individuals with a gambling addiction. In sexual relationships, problems in the sacral chakra can also lead to issues in the heart chakra and vice versa.

Another instance is anxiety that can result from blockages in the root chakra. High levels of anxiety can manifest in various destructive behaviors. Some individuals, for example, try to alleviate their anxiety through seeking pleasure, which can include sexual activity and substance abuse. On the other hand, if you are experiencing issues with your root chakra and do not feel secure and grounded, you may develop anxiety that inhibits your ability to engage in sexual relationships. This may lead to withdrawal and fantasizing. Both chakras can be blocked simultaneously, or problems in the root chakra may even result in a blockage in the sacral chakra.

So, what does a healthy sacral chakra entail? With a healthy sacral chakra, you can easily embrace the various pleasures that life offers without feeling overwhelmed or allowing them to interfere with other aspects of your life. You can fully enjoy sexuality and sexual pleasures while still maintaining balance in your life. Pleasures such as drinking alcohol, savoring good meals, and engaging in sensuality can fill your life without negatively impacting your work or leading to destructive relationships filled with jealousy, multiple partners, and constant drama.

Water is the element closely associated with the sacral chakra. It symbolizes the flow that accompanies healthy pleasure and sensuality. When your sacral chakra is open and healthy, all of your senses are alive and experienced intensely. You can fully enjoy the sense of smell, taste, touch, sight, and sound. The connection with water also represents the flexibility that comes with a healthy sacral chakra. In terms of physical associations, the sacral chakra is connected to the free flow of the lymphatic system, blood, circulatory system, and reproductive fluids.

The flowing nature of the sacral chakra is not only literal in terms of the movement of fluids in the body but also symbolic of the free flow of creative thoughts and fantasies. With a healthy sacral chakra, creative thoughts and ideas effortlessly flow through your mind. Creativity becomes natural and normal. Additionally, the flowing nature of the sacral chakra manifests in flexibility in relationships with others. If your sacral chakra is blocked, your relationships, especially sexual relationships, may be challenging and hindered, as if you constantly encounter resistance. Sexual relationships might dominate your time and energy, even beyond the sexual aspect or any sexual addictions. Conversely, when the sacral chakra is open and healthy, your relationships effortlessly thrive, allowing you to move in and out of them with ease.

Opening the sacral chakra can help you feel and experience the material world more fully by improving your capacity to use all five of your senses.

The pleasures of food, exquisite items and clothes, elegant cars, and other nice things in life may all be experienced when the senses are stimulated, but without overwhelming you. Put another way, another facet of the sacral chakra is the sensation of opulence.

In summary, the sacral chakra is linked to creativity, basic, low-level emotions, pleasure and sensuality, and sexuality.

How Can a Blocked Sacral Chakra Occur?

The sacral chakra can be blocked in various ways. One obvious cause is any form of sexual abuse, rape, or assault, which requires a lengthy and intense process to address the blockage. Another cause can be a dramatic deterioration of an early relationship, especially if it involves betrayal or emotional abuses, thus leading to a blockage of the sacral chakra.

Numerous factors can also contribute to a sacral chakra blockage. For instance, parents with unconventional views on sexuality can pass down these beliefs and hinder the sacral chakra's development in childhood. This phenomenon has become widespread due to puritanical perspectives on sexuality, which still hold influence in Western cultures, fostering a notion that pleasure is "dirty." The impact of this perspective is not always apparent in our consciousness but it can shape our subconscious minds, ultimately resulting in a blockage of the sacral chakra.

The proliferation of pornography is a notable yet challenging topic to discuss. While it is not necessarily wrong to view pornography, it is easy to consume it excessively, leading to a blocked or unbalanced sacral chakra.This consumption can lead to an unhealthy obsession with sexuality or an increased reliance on fantasies, hindering genuine sexual relationships and creating unrealistic standards.Paradoxically, pornography can even numb the sacral chakra, causing a decreased interest in sexuality and pleasure-seeking, leaving individuals unsatisfied. Therefore, caution must be exercised when exposing oneself to this material.

Signs of a Blockage in the Sacral Chakra

In the previous two sections, we mentioned that a blockage in the sacral chakra can have opposite effects. One manifestation of a blocked sacral chakra is feeling disconnected from the world, lacking inspiration, and being unable to experience pleasure. This can lead to a significant decrease in sexual desires or a complete absence of them.

The emotional dullness caused by a blocked sacral chakra can extend to other areas where sensual pleasure is involved. If the blockage is severe, you may find it difficult to enjoy eating and drinking. Food might become uninteresting and tasteless, and although you eat to survive, you won't find enjoyment in it or have much of an appetite.

A blockage in the sacral chakra can also affect the root chakra, resulting in feelings of fear and anxiety. It may lead to avoiding sexual relationships with others and low self-esteem regarding your own sexual attractiveness. Some individuals may even engage in overeating as a subconscious way to make themselves less sexually appealing.

Having a blocked sacral chakra can lead people to unhealthy and abusive relationships, or even prevent them from being involved in relationships at all. Insecurity and low self-esteem caused by the blockage can result in fear, jealousy, and depression. Long-term blockage of the sacral chakra can also lead to depression.

Physical symptoms related to sexuality and reproduction are common signs of a blocked sacral chakra. These symptoms may serve as excuses to avoid sexual relationships, such as frequent urinary tract infections. Men may experience impotence and other performance issues, while women may encounter vaginal dryness and menstruation problems. Both genders can face fertility issues.

Additionally, physical symptoms of a blocked sacral chakra include bladder and kidney stones, gynecological cysts, constipation, and back pain.

If you have a blocked sacral chakra, you may find yourself excessively indulging in fantasies, especially of a sexual nature, accompanied by excessive masturbation. This can hinder your ability to establish and enjoy real-life sexual relationships.Moreover, individuals with a blocked sacral chakra may become so engrossed in fantasies that their creativity in real-life is lost.

Similarly, being alert to an imbalanced sacral chakra is important. Symptoms of an imbalanced sacral chakra involve excessive focus on pleasure-seeking and addictive behaviors. If you engage in activities such as excessive drinking to the point of intoxication, dedicating all free time and money to gambling, having an obsession with food and eating, or being excessively preoccupied with sex, it indicates an imbalance that needs to be addressed to bring the sacral chakra back into harmony.

Appetizers for the Third Eye

Consuming appropriate foods can aid in balancing and restoring harmony to the sacral chakra. It is fortunate that nature offers a wide variety of foods that can support the sacral chakra's healing process. Moreover, these foods often have additional benefits for the root chakra, enabling both chakras to be simultaneously balanced and healed. Furthermore, many of these foods are highly nutritious, promoting overall well-being. When selecting foods for this purpose, it is important to keep the color orange in mind.Carrots and sweet potatoes are examples of foods that benefit both the root and sacral chakra due to their deep orange hues, as well as their grounding and security-enhancing properties as root vegetables. Oranges, orange juice, orange peppers, mangos, orange cantaloupe, peaches, and apricots are also helpful in balancing the sacral chakra. Salmon, in addition to being an excellent source of protein, can contribute to the healing of both the root and sacral chakra. Consuming beef steak can also enhance sexual energy.Almonds and walnuts have been reported to assist in the healing process of the sacral chakra. As the element of the sacral chakra is water, ensuring adequate hydration by consuming enough pure water can be beneficial in maintaining the sacral chakra. Additionally, considering vitamin C supplements can be advantageous.

Aromatherapy for the Sacral Chakra

The application of hot essential oils is beneficial for the sacral chakra, which is connected to sexuality and pleasure. The sacral chakra benefits from sandalwood, which is also good for the root chakra. Orange oil can also be used. Many swear by ylang-ylang, which is also said to have a relaxing effect, to enhance sexual energy. This is going to help you de-stress and let pleasure in. Clary sage has been discovered to be calming and slightly spicy, which will help you become more sensuous. It is especially helpful for senior ladies. A lower back massage and the use of essential oils are also recommended.

The Sacral Chakra's Colors

Bright orange color is intimately related to the sacral chakra. By surrounding oneself with orange, you can enhance your sensual energy. Think about furnishing the bedroom with orange bedspreads, pillowcases, and sheets. Incorporate orange cushions into your meditation area. Donating bright orange apparel items can also enhance your sexual vitality.

For the Sacral Chakra, use crystals

Carnelian is the preferred crystal for the sacral chakra. This stone possesses a vibrant, deep orange color that effectively stimulates the sacral chakra. One can consider placing carnelian stones in their bedroom, either by holding them or incorporating them into meditation, to experience the energy and absorb its benefits.To enhance sensuality, wearing a carnelian pendant or necklace is recommended.

Amber is also suitable for the sacral chakra and can also be utilized for the solar plexus chakra. One can wear jewelry made from amber to benefit from its properties and support these chakras.

Goldstone, a dark orange crystal, is another option for balancing the sacral chakra. Sunstone, tiger's eye, and citrine are also suitable, although they primarily impact the solar plexus chakra due to their yellow color. In conclusion, carnelian is the primary crystal recommended for addressing the sacral chakra.

Practices for Sacral Chakra Meditation

Meditation is a crucial element in the process of healing the sacral chakra. To heal the sacral chakra, it is recommended to surround the meditation space with vibrant orange colors. If possible, meditate during daylight hours, especially in the morning, with open windows that allow plenty of sunlight to enter the room. The meditation for the sacral chakra follows the basic steps described in the previous chapter. Start by sitting in a comfortable position with your eyes closed, taking deep and regular breaths. When meditating for the sacral chakra, slightly tuck your chin down to open up the spine and enhance the flow of energy. Some people suggest meditating in minimal clothing or even nude to experience the sensuality throughout the body. If you are comfortable and have privacy, this can enhance the overall experience.

Begin the meditation by visualizing a radiant white disk in front of you. Take a deep breath and hold it for three to five seconds as you imagine the disk starting to rotate slowly. While it rotates, visualize the disk gradually turning orange and filling up with orange color, spinning faster and generating more energy over time. Now, imagine a ball of bright orange light entering your body and rising slowly towards your root chakra. Visualize the orange disk becoming deeper, brighter, and more energetic as it moves up to the root chakra. Continue visualizing this process until the disk fully transforms into a deep, bright orange color.

Next, imagine the glowing disk moving towards your sacral chakra region, which is located below the navel. Focus your attention on the sacral chakra and the genital area, consciously noticing any sensations that arise, particularly feelings of heat. You can also visualize warm, glowing orange energy enveloping the area of your breasts. Embrace and fully enjoy a healthy and natural sense of sensuality while maintaining control. These meditations will guide you towards achieving this state in your life.

Finally, visualize the orange disk rising into your brain. This will help unleash your creativity and allow for healthy fantasies that are not destructive or obsessive. You can conclude the meditation at this point.

Words of Wisdom for the Sacral Chakra

Using positive statements can assist in balancing and reversing negative thoughts and beliefs about sexuality and sensuality associated with the sacral chakra.

I am capable of acknowledging and managing my emotions without being consumed by them.

- My emotions are powerful and harmonious.
- I experience a relaxed and tranquil state.
- I possess an innate talent for creativity.
- I embrace and willingly share my creative abilities with others.
- I allow emotions to flow freely throughout my entire being.
- I am at peace with my physical self.
- I sense sensuality within my body.
- Sexual experiences are secure and enable me to create meaningful connections.
- I feel safe and secure when engaging in sexual activities.
- I emit an aura of sexuality and sensuality.
- I permit myself to feel at ease.

- I am capable of experiencing pleasure without feeling guilt.
- I have the capacity to fully enjoy and indulge in all the pleasures life brings.
- My enjoyment of meals is heightened and profound.
- I attract individuals who share a healthy view of sexuality and possess similar mindsets.
- I am capable of expressing my sexuality in a positive and healthy manner.
- I derive pleasure from life's passions without becoming overwhelmed by them.

5

Chakra of the Solar Plexus

As we ascend the chakras, we transition from more emotional and "animal" elements of ourselves to more mature and ultimately spiritually oriented traits. There are several traits associated with the solar plexus chakra that we anticipate people to start exhibiting in their teenage and young adult years. These are the qualities that will make you successful at job or in an educational setting. Consider the solar plexus chakra as providing you with the self-assurance and determination you require to complete tasks, look after yourself, and look out for others.

An explanation of the Solar Plexus Chakra

CHAKRA OF THE SOLAR PLEXUS

The solar plexus chakra is located in the central abdominal area, above the navel and below the rib cage. It is a higher energy chakra compared to the root and sacral chakras and is associated with the color yellow. It is important to note that we are referring to the spiritual aspects of energy, rather than the physical intensity felt in the body. The solar plexus chakra operates at a higher level and vibrates at a higher frequency than the root and sacral chakras. It consists of 10 lotus petals and is commonly associated with the element of fire. In Sanskrit, it is referred to as Manipura.

However, the solar plexus chakra is still considered a matter chakra because it is associated with earthly concerns rather than spiritual matters, although it has more of an intellectual nature.

The main theme of the solar plexus chakra is empowerment, particularly in one's interactions with others. While it is not specifically linked to work, it greatly influences work and career. Individuals who are successful in their work usually have a strong and open solar plexus chakra.

Having a healthy and open solar plexus chakra gives one a sense of self-confidence in the work environment and when collaborating on projects with others, even within a family setting. It comes naturally to take the lead and express creative ideas that originate from the sacral chakra. Individuals also take responsibility for their plans and actions.

In essence, the solar plexus chakra embodies the characteristics of a leader. Historical figures like Catherine the Great, Napoleon, Patton, and Caesar all possessed a strong and healthy solar plexus chakra. However, the actual use of confidence and leadership abilities depends on other factors. The solar plexus chakra generates confidence and willpower, but it does not guarantee their positive use.

A healthy solar plexus chakra facilitates the ease of executing plans and self-discipline becomes a natural trait. This highlights the importance of balance.When one is out of balance, particularly with the sacral chakra, they may lack the self-discipline associated with the solar plexus chakra. Self-discipline is often necessary to work hard and achieve career goals, which may require sacrificing immediate pleasures. Engaging in pleasures is appropriate when it does not hinder professional success.

The root chakra is connected to fulfilling basic needs and financial security, while the solar plexus chakra is associated with wealth building. This is because accumulating wealth requires confidence in executing plans. Some people suggest using yellow carved stones shaped like money trees to help balance the solar plexus chakra. The solar plexus chakra is strongly linked to wealth and abundance.

Having a mindset of wealth and abundance is possible in any job or career where one excels, or as an independent entrepreneur.It is not necessary to have the best job. Having a healthy solar plexus chakra means being disciplined enough to effectively save and invest money, and constantly working towards personal wealth. A person with a healthy solar plexus chakra does not compare their wealth to others, but focuses on accumulating wealth suitable for their own situation.

A healthy solar plexus chakra brings clarity and purpose to one's work and career, as well as their role at home. They have clear vision and sound judgment, trusting their decisions without self-doubt. With an open and healthy solar plexus chakra, they are confident in speaking up and leading others. Strong solar plexus chakra often correlates with intellectual and analytical abilities, which can be observed in creative individuals such as authors, artists, and even passionate cooks who create recipe sites. However, not everyone with creative talents achieves success, while others turn their passion into a full-time living.

It is important to consider the connection between the sacral chakra and the solar plexus chakra in assessing the health of the latter. If the sacral chakra is functioning reasonably well, the individual may have many creative ideas and plans that fail to materialize or struggle to be implemented.

If you possess a robust solar plexus chakra, you will possess confidence and strength when it comes to your beliefs and opinions. However, this does not imply being forceful or assertive about them. Individuals who are pushy with their beliefs often reveal inner feelings of insecurity. When plagued with insecurity, you are likely to struggle with becoming agitated and emotional when faced with challenges to your beliefs or presented with differing opinions. Conversely, an individual with a healthy solar plexus chakra will display inner confidence and tranquility, allowing this confidence to shine through in the face of challenges without becoming emotional or demeaning others.

Having an open solar plexus chakra will result in a sense of ease and effortlessness. This does not mean that you will not have to devote hard work or energy to your projects, but rather that your efforts will flow naturally. Individuals with a healthy solar plexus chakra possess an intuitive understanding of what needs to be done in order to plan and execute any endeavor. Moreover, they may emit a contagious level of energy that impacts others.

How Does a Blocked Solar Plexus Chakra Occur?

Childhood experiences that erode our confidence can result in a blocked solar plexus chakra. This blockage can be caused by well-intentioned but harsh mentors or teachers who employ negative language and belittling tactics in an attempt to motivate children to work harder. Instead of assisting the child, these actions diminish their self-assurance, leaving them with low self-esteem and eliminating their innate positive attitude.

It is not limited to childhood, as individuals can also be affected by this phenomenon when someone important to them engages in criticism or doubts their abilities, leading to diminished self-confidence.This self-doubt creates an energy that obstructs the solar plexus chakra.

The impact of life's inevitable setbacks on the solar plexus chakra can vary depending on the overall balance of the chakras and the individual's constitution. If a person starts from a position of strength, they can easily recover from failures. If all three of the lower chakras (root, sacral, and solar plexus) are open and in harmony, a major failure prompts analysis, planning, and learning from the experience to be applied in the future. However, if there are existing blockages or imbalances, a project failure can completely obstruct the solar plexus chakra.

Furthermore, our reactions to failure can be influenced by those around us, whether it is in a professional, personal, or educational setting. There are individuals who use the failure of others as an opportunity to belittle them. Being subjected to such behavior can further contribute to the blockage of the solar plexus chakra.

Signs of a Blockage in the Solar Plexus Chakra

When considering symptoms of a solar plexus chakra, one should think about the opposite of what has been previously discussed. If someone's solar plexus chakra is open and functioning properly, they will exhibit self-confidence and eagerness to take on and complete projects.However, if their solar plexus chakra is blocked, they may be inclined to avoid responsibility and lack the confidence to speak out or express their opinions. Furthermore, individuals with a blocked solar plexus chakra may struggle with self-doubt and have difficulty completing projects. This lack of certainty may even extend to their beliefs and opinions.

A blocked solar plexus chakra can also lead to a mindset of scarcity or a poverty mentality. This doesn't necessarily mean financial instability, but rather a fixed belief that the current level of wealth is all that can be achieved and that prosperity is merely a matter of chance. Consequently, this mindset hinders individuals from taking action to improve their financial situation, resigning themselves to the status quo.It is not uncommon for a poverty mentality to correlate with a blocked root chakra, producing a subconscious belief that there is never enough money.

In addition, having a blocked solar plexus chakra can impair one's ability to demonstrate self-discipline and be an effective leader.Individuals may prioritize immediate gratification over hard work and may struggle to bring creative projects to completion. Individuals who possess a healthy sacral chakra but a blocked solar plexus often find themselves surrounded by unfinished endeavors, unable to effectively guide others.

Lastly, individuals with a blocked solar plexus chakra may struggle to maintain boundaries due to their lack of self-discipline. Separating work from leisure becomes challenging, which contrasts with the high level of self-discipline required for entrepreneurial success.Consequently, individuals with a blocked solar plexus chakra may feel stuck and unable to make progress in their endeavors.

Detachment and Absence of Intent

Apathy and a lack of purpose are commonly linked to a blocked solar plexus. The level of apathy varies among individuals, but when the solar plexus chakra is blocked, one may become indifferent towards work and their overall work life. While in school, it may be difficult to find satisfaction or develop a passion for anything. Those with a blocked solar plexus chakra who attend college often switch majors frequently.This is because they feel apathetic towards any subject they try and lack the commitment to see anything through to completion. It wouldn't be surprising if they struggle to graduate, and if they do, it would likely be due to simply getting by rather than finding a genuine passion.

In addition to the lack of purpose in life, there may also be spiritual blockages present. Nevertheless, when the solar plexus chakra is blocked, the absence of purpose is primarily related to one's occupation or career. This is accompanied by a lack of interest and effort towards work, where the individual only does what is necessary to avoid being fired, but nothing more.

Overzealous Solar Plexus

Similar to what we've observed with the sacral chakra, the solar plexus chakra can also become imbalanced and overactive. One example of this is the workaholic personality, where individuals with an overactive solar plexus chakra dedicate excessive amounts of time to work and money-making. They prioritize long hours at the office over meeting their basic human needs for pleasure and relaxation. These individuals will always find a reason to stay late at work, often neglecting their partners, families, and personal wellbeing. The excessive workload can lead to health issues such as ulcers, digestive problems, and even serious conditions like heart disease and cancer.

Interestingly, individuals with an overactive solar plexus chakra tend to be very frugal. Since this chakra is associated with wealth and abundance, when it becomes overactive and imbalanced, individuals may develop a mindset that excessively values money for its own sake. They become unwilling to spend money, even on necessary expenses. Despite having a high income, they become fixated on saving every penny. They will use coupons, refuse to lend money, and drive old, worn-out cars. They also tend to judge harshly those who enjoy luxury items or take vacations. If these individuals never find healing, they will likely take their wealth to the grave with them.

Food for the Chakra of the Solar Plexus

Foods with vibrant yellow hues can aid in the healing of the solar plexus chakra. Begin with squash. Use lemon to add flavor to your food and beverages. Include yellow bell peppers in your salads. Consume corn or corn chips or tacos with yellow corn shells. The solar plexus chakra can be opened with the use of golden apples. Eating pasta, lentils, and oats can also benefit the solar plexus chakra. Additionally helpful are regular potatoes and lots of butter, particularly grass-fed butter, which will have a vibrant, deep yellow color.

Essential Oils for Chakra of the Solar Plexus

Lemon oil is the best essential oil to use for treating the solar plexus. Still, a lot of different oils have their uses. These consist of ginger, cinnamon oil, and chamomile. Clove oil is recommended by certain essential oil practitioners for the solar plexus chakra.

The Solar Plexus Chakra's colors

Bright yellow hues are obviously beneficial for mending the solar plexus chakra. Additionally, you can mix white and yellow. Bring as much sunshine into your living area as you can, especially in the mornings, late afternoons, and early evenings as dusk draws near. Fill your life with these hues. When it's essential, try painting a room a bright yellow color to be used for solar plexus chakra meditation in addition to using yellow pillows and bed linens.

Crystals for the Chakra of the Solar Plexus

You can use a variety of yellow-colored gemstones and stones to assist in the healing of the solar plexus chakra. One of the most well-liked crystals is citrine. By using stones that overlap with the solar plexus chakra, you may balance and heal both at the same time when healing the sacral chakra. For this aim, try utilizing amber; tiger's eye is also beneficial for both chakras. The solar plexus chakra can also be healed by yellow jasper and yellow topaz, among other stones.

Chakra Meditation for the Solar Plexus

To practice meditation for the solar plexus chakra, assume a comfortable sitting position and close your eyes, taking deep breaths. Meditating in the morning or evening can be beneficial for the solar plexus chakra, especially if you can do it outside or near a window where sunlight is present. The solar plexus chakra is closely connected to the sun's yellow energy. However, if meditating in the sun is not feasible for you, do not worry.

During the meditation, visualize a spinning wheel of vibrant yellow light. While focusing on the solar plexus chakra, imagine this light passing through the root and sacral chakras on its journey. Try to envision the light becoming brighter and more energetic as it ascends into the location of the solar plexus chakra. As you inhale, visualize the light expanding, and as you exhale, see it shrink. Devote approximately 15 minutes per day to meditating on this chakra.

As mentioned earlier, if you have the opportunity to meditate in the sun during the morning or evening hours, it can be particularly helpful. You will be able to feel and absorb the comforting energy of the sun's yellow light while meditating.

For the Solar Plexus Chakra: Affirmations

There are many aspects related to the solar plexus chakra that occur at a subconscious level, and in this case, daily affirmations can be particularly useful. To begin, the following affirmations can aid in this process:
1. I possess strength and confidence.
2. I have the determination to complete whatever I start.
3. I am a leader and can comfortably establish the path for others.
4. I deserve to have my ideas listened to and respected.
5. I am a creative individual capable of transforming my visions into reality.
6. The intense yellow energy emitted by the sun awakens my spirit.

7. I will direct the powerful yellow energy from the sun towards a creative purpose.

8. I take pleasure in my ability to manifest and bring things into fruition.

9. I have unwavering faith in my own capabilities and feel self-sufficient.

10. My body is infused with the energy required to accomplish all of my projects.

11. I am capable of devising plans and transforming them into tangible results.

12. I am brimming with personal power.

13. I am intelligent and possess sound judgment.

14. I can assert my desires without causing harm to others.

15. I possess the ability to accurately assess any given situation.

16. I exhibit the qualities of a leader and a decision-maker.

17. I hold the reins of my own life.

18. I am attracting wealth and abundance into my life.

6

Chakra of the Heart

This chapter marks the beginning of our exploration into the spiritual realm. Here, we encounter the heart chakra. From a technical standpoint, it is not typically considered a spiritual chakra and is rather seen as intermediate, bridging the gap between the physical chakras and the spiritual chakras. The heart chakra is associated with love, acceptance, and empathy. These emotions and states of being extend beyond various boundaries. In some ways, romantic love is a rather basic emotion. Although many individuals experience romantic love, it often remains in an immature state. In such cases, despite having feelings for another person, romantic love tends to be self-centered and can even be selfish. In its immature state, romantic love can frequently manifest as possessiveness over another individual. However, when one has yet to reach certain levels of growth and maturity, it is entirely true that romantic love can mean loving someone more than oneself and coming together as a unified entity. Therefore, it is evident that the heart chakra encompasses both the physical and spiritual aspects when examining the dynamics of romantic love. The emotional components can be primitive and ego-driven, but they can also be selfless in their nature. This demonstrates that the heart chakra encompasses both the material and spiritual realms. It possesses numerous elements that extend far beyond romantic love. To develop these aspects and fully unlock the potential of the heart chakra, one must first heal the root chakra, the sacral chakra, and the solar plexus chakra. At its core, the heart chakra involves self-love and self-acceptance. The emotions of empathy, tolerance, and understanding towards others emerge from the heart chakra. Therefore, it is evident that the power of the heart chakra encompasses love and understanding towards all of humanity, and indeed, all of life itself.

The Heart Chakra: What Is It?

The heart chakra is situated at the center of the chest. Its color is green, which is an appropriate representation of its energy level. The green color indicates that the heart chakra vibrates at a higher frequency compared to the solar plexus and lower chakras. Occasionally, the heart chakra may also emit pink colors, indicating a resonance with romantic love. In Sanskrit, the heart chakra is known as Anahata. It is depicted as a green flower with 12 lotus petals.

The foundation of a healthy heart chakra lies in self-love. Without self-love, it becomes difficult to share love with others and genuinely love them. Showing love to others includes prioritizing their needs, sometimes even more than our own. The heart chakra is closely associated with love, relationships, and friendship. The heart chakra is most strongly felt during moments of romantic love, often causing intense sensations and even pain in the center of the chest.

However, the heart chakra also relates to forms of love beyond the romantic. Unconditional love for one's children, depicted by green colors, is a function of the heart chakra. Love experienced in friendships also stems from the heart chakra, although it might be less intense. Love for pets and animals is also associated with the heart chakra.

The heart chakra also encompasses genuine love, compassion, and empathy towards all people and living beings. This love operates differently and is characterized by compassion for all life. Consequently, it emanates from the heart chakra.

The heart chakra encompasses even more than what has been said. Many attributes and emotions are linked to the heart chakra, operating at a higher level. Understanding the heart chakra becomes clearer when all the chakras are studied, as it is often described as a connecting point between the physical and spiritual chakras. For this reason, the state of the heart chakra plays a role in how one copes with and recovers from illnesses and setbacks in life. When the heart chakra is open and healed, managing stress becomes easier, and recovery from illnesses is swifter. Conversely, unchecked illness and stress can have negative effects on the heart chakra.

The painful experience of losing a loved one brings forth intense grief. In the process of grieving, we must come to terms with our loss and find peace. The heart chakra is central to this process, allowing us to both experience and express grief, as well as helping us find acceptance. Those who have developed spiritually understand that life continues beyond the physical body, making it easier for them to come to terms with the grief of losing someone.

While the root, sacral, and solar plexus chakras are associated with the self, the heart chakra is seen as a chakra that establishes connections. It enables the exchange of energy with other forms of life, from tiny flowers to people and spirits. When the heart chakra is open and healed, relating to others becomes effortless, and relationships are harmonious and free of difficulties.

The heart chakra plays a role in integrating thoughts and emotions, leading to a deeper understanding of wisdom rather than just creativity. When the heart chakra is open, the creativity stemming from the sacral chakra becomes more significant. It also has an impact on the solar plexus chakra, which contributes to confidence and decisive leadership. However, an open heart chakra is essential for being a good leader, as it fosters empathy, compassion, and the ability to consider others' ideas and feelings. Leaders with an open heart chakra create teams where everyone feels valued. The heart chakra is responsible for the appreciation of beauty, elevating pleasure and luxury to a higher level. If you can appreciate art or music deeply, it signifies a developed and open heart chakra.

Having an open heart chakra allows for a carefree existence, where empathy and compassion are natural. Connecting with others and building bridges becomes effortless.Trust is easily established, and giving to others brings a sense of fulfillment rather than loss. In romantic relationships, an open heart chakra fosters an ease devoid of drama, jealousy, and hurt. Conflicts may arise, but they can be resolved easily.

Acceptance and forgiveness are crucial signs of a healthy heart chakra. With an open heart chakra, forgiveness comes without difficulty and is genuine. However, it is important to maintain balance with the solar plexus chakra, which protects against exploitation and being taken advantage of. Therefore, forgiveness should not be extended to those who do not show genuine change or improvement.

The heart chakra is associated with the concept of "connection," and its corresponding element is air. This symbolizes the free flow of love energy among all living beings, emphasizing the interconnectedness of everything.Additionally, the ability to change and adapt is a characteristic of a healthy heart chakra. It allows for transformation when necessary, rather than being rigid and stuck in one's ways.

How Can a Block in the Heart Chakra Occur?

There are various ways in which the heart chakra can become obstructed. The heart chakra may become blocked if love is inconsistent or withheld during childhood. A child's heart chakra can be blocked if one parent leaves the family.Although divorce can be traumatic for a child, it will not have a lasting impact on the heart chakra if the other parent remains loving and engaged in the child's life.

Rejection at any point in life can result in a blocked heart chakra, and the likelihood of blockage increases with younger age and less emotional maturity. Rejection by friends can significantly affect the heart chakra, particularly if it occurs between the ages of 6 and 13. Additionally, a failure to be accepted during the teenage years can also block the heart chakra.

Betrayal-based rejection has an especially profound impact on the heart chakra. It can occur in romantic relationships, as well as in work relationships or friendships.Any experience that erodes trust and limits connectivity with others can block the heart chakra. It is important to note that the younger one is when betrayed, the higher the chances of a blocked heart chakra. However, this can happen at any age.

Similar to other chakras, balance is crucial when considering the heart chakra. An imbalanced heart chakra can lead to dysfunctional behaviors, which can be equally significant as a blocked heart chakra depending on the circumstances.

Heart Chakra Blockage Symptoms

The symptoms associated with a blocked heart chakra are connected to feelings of connectivity and the ability to establish and maintain relationships of all types.It's important to note that the heart chakra affects relationships beyond just romantic ones, including those with parents, siblings, friends, and even animals.

When the heart chakra is blocked due to negative experiences or rejection during childhood or adolescence, it can lead to social anxiety in adulthood. If someone is extremely shy, it could suggest that their heart chakra was blocked during the formative years of ages 3-8 or during emotionally intense teenage years. However, it is possible to open and heal a blocked heart chakra, and the first step is self-awareness to initiate corrective action.

Individuals with blocked heart chakras may exhibit various manifestations. Some may feel lonely and disconnected, while others may harbor resentment, hold grudges, and lack forgiveness. Consequently, a blocked chakra may result in an inability to feel empathy and compassion, with a tendency to be self-centered in relations with others.Although people with blocked heart chakras may still engage in romantic relationships and have many social contacts, their perspective on these relationships is primarily self-focused, lacking spiritual development.

This type of blockage in the heart chakra can lead to feelings of jealousy and anger. Additionally, it may indicate a lack of self-confidence stemming from a blocked or underdeveloped solar plexus chakra. In such cases, individuals may partake in romantic relationships and experience intense emotions, but their minds will be plagued with paranoid thoughts and a constant need to check up on their partner. Even the smallest indication can trigger jealous and angry feelings, driven by fear, suspicion of cheating, or a belief that the other party doesn't reciprocate love, regardless of any actual signs of affection.

In contrast, some individuals with a blocked heart chakra express it through a lack of empathy. They may adopt a highly judgmental and critical stance towards others, lacking compassion and exhibiting a disinclination to donate to charity. In the workplace, they may perceive themselves as superior to their colleagues.

A blocked heart chakra can hinder one's ability to give freely to others. If they do engage in acts of giving or sharing, it may be done with the expectation of something in return or to seek acknowledgment, ultimately serving to boost their own self-esteem and public image.

For many, a blocked heart chakra leads to emotional withdrawal and reservation. They may abstain from romantic relationships altogether and have few friends, rarely socializing with them. In extreme cases, they may even distance themselves from immediate family members.Some individuals experience a blocked heart chakra after the death of their parents, resulting in their withdrawal from other family members and friends, with work being their main source of social interaction.

Physical symptoms can also arise from a blocked heart chakra, such as indigestion, heartburn, high blood pressure, chest pains, and shoulder pains. In severe cases, it can even lead to heart disease. Medical professionals acknowledge that social disconnect can contribute to heart disease, so it's important to seek immediate medical attention if experiencing chest pains.

In summary, a blocked heart chakra can profoundly impact various aspects of an individual's life, but it is possible to address and heal it through self-awareness and taking corrective action.

An Excessive Heart Chakra

In the past, we have observed that having an excessively active chakra can be just as detrimental as having a blocked chakra. For instance, when the sacral chakra is overactive, it can lead to issues such as sexual addiction, alcohol consumption, drug abuse, and gambling.Similarly, an overactive heart chakra can also have negative consequences. When the heart chakra is out of balance, similar to the sacral chakra, the qualities associated with the heart chakra can be expressed excessively.

Let's consider the emotion of love and caring for others.It is crucial to find a balance between caring for oneself and caring for the other person in any type of love relationship. In a healthy relationship, you not only consider the needs of the other person but also pay attention to your own needs. Assuming you have a healthy level of self-confidence, you will be able to communicate your own needs to your partner or friend. Additionally, we understand that compromise and maintaining a balance are essential aspects of a healthy relationship.

However, when the heart chakra becomes overactive, the boundary between oneself and others can blur and disappear completely. In severe cases, individuals may lose their sense of identity entirely. In such situations, individuals may neglect their own needs entirely and solely focus on meeting the needs of others. This can be seen as complete selflessness or having a "Mother Theresa" complex.While many people may admire individuals like Mother Theresa who dedicated their lives to helping others, for most of us, it is an unhealthy approach to interpersonal relationships.Neglecting oneself entirely to serve humanity is not a constructive way to contribute.

Individuals with an overactive heart chakra may not exhibit such extreme behaviors but often find themselves consistently involved in codependent relationships. Healthy adults do not build their relationships on codependency. Instead, both individuals contribute to each other's needs while being capable of taking care of themselves independently. A healthy relationship brings two independent souls together to create something greater than the sum of their parts. In a codependent relationship, there exists a needy child-like person and another individual with an overactive heart chakra who assumes the role of a parental figure. In this type of relationship, the person with the overactive heart chakra primarily focuses on fulfilling the needs of the other person while neglecting their own needs.

Another symptom of an overactive heart chakra is an excessive willingness to trust others. Trust is crucial for establishing connections with people; however, there are many untrustworthy individuals in the world who engage in stealing, cheating, and causing harm. When a person lacks proper discernment, they may enter into relationships with such individuals, causing them various forms of harm. People with an overactive heart chakra often find themselves too willing to trust and accept others, leading to suffering when those unworthy of trust become intimately involved in their lives and cause damage.

Furthermore, individuals with an overactive heart chakra tend to say yes to everything. They may continuously give others money, even at their own detriment. They may also neglect their own health, exercise, and personal time because they always prioritize the needs of others.Although this can impact both genders, women are more prone to being the "yes" person more frequently than men.

Another sign of an overactive heart chakra is frequently and easily getting involved in romantic relationships. These individuals may find themselves falling in love frequently and quickly moving from one person to another. In contrast, when the heart chakra is open, healthy, and balanced, falling in love should not occur easily. These individuals are open to love but exercise discrimination and caution.

In conclusion, an overactive heart chakra is associated with the complete erosion of the ego and self.

Recipes to Open the Heart Chakra

Foods with a green hue are especially beneficial for the heart chakra. Green veggies, such as spinach, broccoli, and green beans, are edible. Avocados and olive oil are also options. Green peppers and olives are also delicious. For this reason, you can basically include any green vegetable in your meals. Kiwi is another green fruit that, combined with lime, can aid in the healing of the heart chakra. Consider creative ways to include lime in your diet. Foods high in energy, such as red meat varieties, can also be beneficial. Considering this, think of salmon. It is also acceptable to eat prime rib and pork for this reason.

Essential Oils for Chakra of the Heart

In order to restore the heart chakra, consider rekindling compassion and a sense of connection. You can use rose oil to open up and strengthen your heart chakra. Rose oil has a pleasant aroma that can assist to relax the mind and promote feelings of joy, empathy, and openness to the heart. With its zesty aromas, neroli oil will assist you in creating a solid foundation for the heart chakra, which will allow it to open without causing you to lose your identity. Because of its green hue, marjoram is another beneficial essential oil to utilize for healing in cases when your heart chakra has been blocked by traumatic experiences.

The Heart Chakra's Colors

Green hues are the ones you want to surround yourself with in order to cure the heart chakra. You can work with different shades of green, and wearing green clothes and wearing green crystals (see below) can be beneficial. To encourage the green energy connected to the heart chakra, use green pillows, draperies, and linens.

Crystals for the Chakra of the Heart

The heart chakra can be worked with a variety of crystals, such as jade and green emerald. What components of the heart chakra are most bothering you can influence your color choice. If the issue is found generally in nature, stay with stones that are naturally green in color. Rose quartz can help with healing if your issues are mainly related to romantic love.

Heart Chakra Meditation

The color green will be the main theme of the heart chakra meditation. As is customary, adopt the relaxed stance. Visualize a green ball of light approaching you. Imagine it expanding until it reaches your size and is there in front of you. Observe the green light coming through your nose and filling your entire chest with energy each time you breathe in. Feel the love, connection, trust, and empathy that the green energy carries when you do this. For 15 to 20 minutes, see yourself breathing in the green light. Breathe in and out for five seconds each time.

Positive Spells for the Heart Chakra

Affirmations targeted at the heart chakra can aid in rejuvenating one's sense of self and bolstering the confidence required for healthy, nurturing relationships.

- I have a deep affection and connection towards other individuals.
- I place trust in others, yet expect them to earn it.
- I am deserving of love and respect.
- I greatly enjoy socializing and being in the company of loved ones.
- I will generously extend assistance to others without any expectation of reciprocity.
- While I am willing to assist others, I will not permit it to cause harm or distress to myself.
- The love I experience for all living beings is limitless and filled with immense joy.
- I am receptive to expressing love towards others.
- I grant myself forgiveness for any mistakes I have made.
- I love myself unconditionally.
- I am open to receiving love from others.
- I wholeheartedly and unreservedly forgive others.
- I possess profound compassion for others and empathy towards their suffering.
- Upon meeting my own needs, I will dedicate a portion of my life towards aiding others.

7

Grasping Chakra

The first chakra that is genuinely spiritual is the throat chakra. It is not advisable to work on the throat chakra until the other chakras that we have discussed are balanced and healed. Therefore, please focus on clearing the root, sacral, solar plexus, and heart chakras before addressing the throat chakra.

The Throat Chakra: What Is It?

The throat chakra is situated in the lower front part of the throat and is the origin of speech. It is referred to as Vishuddha in Sanskrit and is associated with the color blue, often depicted as aquamarine or turquoise. This chakra's vibrational energy is considered higher than that of the other chakras we have studied. Blue light has a higher energy level than green light, which is higher than yellow light, and so on. As one becomes more spiritually inclined, the energy of vibration increases, resulting in the blue to purple range for spiritual chakras. The heart chakra, serving as a connection between the matter and spiritual chakras, is green, representing a blend of blue and yellow energies.

The number of petals on a flower used to symbolize a chakra also reflects higher energy states. In the case of the throat chakra, there are sixteen lotus petals. The spiritual chakras differ in complexity due to their spiritual nature. It is important to understand the dimensionality of the universe before delving into the spiritual chakras. Our physical universe consists of four dimensions - three for physical movement and one for time. However, scientists suggest the existence of additional dimensions, potentially 11, 13, or even 26, where psychic and spiritual energies are found, and where deceased individuals may reside.

Given its spiritual nature, the throat chakra extends slightly beyond the physical body, although its location is centered in the throat area. The throat chakra is primarily associated with information, truth, and communication. In spiritual terms, it serves as a link between your inner spirit and the material world, allowing you to vocalize your inner thoughts and ideas to others. As such, the throat chakra facilitates connections with people in various types of interactions, including romantic, sexual, creative, and professional relationships. It interacts with the heart, sacral, solar plexus, and sacral chakras depending on the context.

Speaking the truth, as well as one's truth, is a crucial aspect of the throat chakra. It is also involved in expressing oneself appropriately and engaging in nonverbal communication. Similar to the solar plexus chakra's role in transforming creative ideas into reality, the throat chakra is equally important in this regard due to its significance in effective communication. If ideas cannot be communicated truthfully, they are unlikely to be realized. The throat chakra is also closely connected to a sense of purpose in work and career, working in tandem with the solar plexus chakra. Opening the throat chakra enhances communication with others, making it an essential component in combining creativity, determination, and vision.

How Does a Blocked Throat Chakra Occur?

A blockage in the throat chakra may arise from unfavorable experiences related to sharing your opinions or facts. Again, the effects will be profound if this occurs throughout childhood or adolescence. When a child comes to parents or guardians with ideas or the truth, it can be extremely harmful and block the throat chakra if the adult mocks the child. When you get older and people make fun of or ignore your ideas and thoughts, the throat chakra might get blocked. That can be a powerful tool in the hands of abusive people.

Signs of an obstruction in the throat chakra

A blockage in the throat chakra can lead to difficulties in communication with others.This can manifest in various ways such as feeling too shy to speak in groups or unable to express true feelings and needs in intimate situations. If you find yourself excessively afraid of speaking, it may be a sign of a blocked throat chakra. This can occur in social situations, one-on-one interactions, or at work. It is also possible for this type of blockage to be connected to a blocked solar plexus chakra, as the solar plexus is associated with self-confidence. In such cases, it is advisable to meditate on both chakras.

Another indication of a blocked throat chakra is speaking in low volumes.

Do people often say they can't hear you or fail to hear you at all? People with a blocked throat chakra may perceive this as being ignored when in reality, others are simply unaware of their speech. This usually happens in social settings with three or more people or in a work environment. Feeling ignored can exacerbate the blockage and cause additional anxieties in social situations, potentially affecting the heart chakra. The sensation of being disregarded when attempting to vocalize ideas can lead to feelings of devaluation, lower self-esteem, and reduced self-confidence, thereby blocking the solar plexus chakra. The throat chakra plays a crucial role in our interactions with others and how we perceive these interactions, so if it becomes blocked, it can trigger blockages in multiple chakras.

Conversely, the health of the solar plexus chakra and the heart chakra also impact the throat chakra. If you lack confidence or feel socially disconnected, it can weaken even an open throat chakra, leading to potential blockages as situations progress.

It is important to note that a blocked throat chakra not only affects your ability to speak but also has a negative impact on your character. Furthermore, your character is revealed through your speech habits. For instance, individuals who frequently lie often have a blocked throat chakra, as this chakra is closely linked to the ability to speak truthfully.

Keeping your word is another significant aspect of your personality connected to the throat chakra. If you struggle to fulfill your commitments, people will find it difficult to trust you and your words, promises, or agreements will lose credibility. Most people consider this to be a serious character flaw. If your throat chakra is blocked, you are more likely to engage in such behavior, where you say one thing but do another, or make agreements and fail to uphold them.

Other character flaws indicating a blocked throat chakra include a tendency to gossip or an inability to keep secrets. If you frequently divulge personal information about others or spread rumors impulsively, it is likely a result of a blocked throat chakra.

Another classic symptom of a blocked throat chakra is mumbling while speaking. In this case, your voice may be audible enough, but subconsciously you alter the use of your mouth and tongue in dysfunctional ways that hinder others from understanding your speech.

A blocked throat chakra may lead to saying inappropriate things or speaking in a way that is unsuitable for the current situation. Additionally, it can manifest as using speech to belittle others or make them feel bad. This blockage affects all forms of communication, including writing. Therefore, the words we write, whether in emails, text messages, or on paper, may be influenced by a blocked throat chakra. On the other hand, an overactive throat chakra can cause a person to become a loud and attention-seeking speaker. This behavior may stem from underlying insecurities or a desire to dominate conversations, thereby hindering others from expressing themselves. In some cases, an overactive throat chakra can result in an inability to listen to others, leading to strained relationships or a lack of acknowledgement for other people's ideas and concerns. Moreover, it may even prevent individuals from being consciously aware that others are trying to communicate with them. When assessing our chakras, it is important not to shy away from recognizing our own flaws. Seeing ourselves in these characteristics does not make us bad people; rather, it highlights areas where we can improve. It is crucial to remember that blocked chakras can be a result of the upbringing provided by parents, guardians, or caregivers during our formative years, so we should not blame ourselves for their occurrence. Nonetheless, the fact that we are actively studying chakras and engaging in practices such as meditation and yoga indicates that we are on the path to healing.

Manifestations of a Blocked Throat Chakra Physically

Symptoms related to a blocked throat chakra often revolve around speech difficulties.Laryngitis is a common issue among individuals with a blocked throat chakra. Unexplained sore throats are also associated with a blocked throat chakra.A scratchy or dry throat is a common manifestation, accompanied by a constant need to clear one's throat.Neck pain and oral issues may arise as a result. Biting the tongue frequently can lead to discomfort and soreness, indicating a blocked throat chakra. Dental problems like toothaches may also be a possible symptom. In some cases, chronic sinus problems or allergies can make communication more challenging. It is not uncommon to experience hand or wrist pain, which can hinder activities like typing or texting on a computer. Essentially, any difficulty in speaking clearly or comprehensibly, particularly if it is chronic or recurrent, suggests a blocked throat chakra. When severe physical problems arise, it is advisable to seek medical attention for immediate treatment. However, addressing the blocked throat chakra is necessary to resolve the long-term energetic issues causing these problems in the first place.

Foods for Chakra of the Throat

Numerous meals are beneficial for maintaining and healing the throat chakra. Although foods with a purple hue also help, you should seek for foods with a blue hue. In addition to their many health advantages, blueberries and blackberries are great foods that can support the healing of the throat chakra. Any shade of dark grape can also aid in the healing of the throat chakra. You can also incorporate purple potato varieties into your diet to aid in the healing of the throat chakra.

Essential Oils for Chakra of the Throat

When using essential oils to treat the throat chakra, it is important to select calming varieties that can alleviate sore throats. It is also beneficial to choose oils that can promote and improve overall well-being. Geranium is a suitable option for sore throats and is often utilized for this purpose. Another effective choice is jasmine oil, which has been recognized for its ability to address issues related to a hoarse voice. Blocked throat chakras often result in hoarseness, making jasmine oil a valuable remedy for individuals with persistent hoarseness.

When working on healing the throat chakra with essential oils, it is essential to consider that the throat chakra is a spiritual chakra with a relatively high level of energetic vibration. As a result, frankincense is a recommended oil to use for throat chakra healing due to its elevated energetic frequency and its spiritual and sacred properties.

The Throat Chakra's Colors

The throat chakra is often associated with the colors blue and aquamarine. Turquoise is also a beneficial color for healing the throat chakra. To promote healing, you can decorate your living space using a range of blue shades, from lighter to darker tones. The spiritual energy of the colors becomes stronger as the blue shade darkens and the green components decrease. Therefore, it is advisable to choose appropriate shades based on the specific manifestation of a blocked throat chakra. For instance, darker colors are preferable if the blockage is linked to character issues like gossiping, lying, or not keeping promises. On the other hand, lighter shades and blue-green mixtures like aquamarine and turquoise are suitable if the blockage expresses itself through speaking insecurities or suppressing communication. In most cases, a combination of these colors is recommended to address all consciousness aspects connected to the throat chakra during the healing process. Additionally, wearing blue-colored clothing can aid in throat chakra healing. Whether you are practicing meditation, yoga, or going about your day, incorporating blue into your attire can be beneficial.

Crystals for the Chakra of the Throat

There are numerous beneficial crystals that can assist in the healing of the throat chakra. These crystals, with their vibrant and pleasing colors, are often utilized in jewelry to enhance the energetic frequency of an open throat chakra.Much like the impact of the colors one wears or surrounds oneself with, different types of stones and crystals can be chosen to influence the energetic vibrational range of the throat chakra.

One such crystal that aids in the healing of the throat chakra is turquoise, an incredibly beautiful stone. It can be worn and is commonly used in jewelry.Alternatively, one can spend time observing and holding large turquoise stones, allowing the calming energy to envelop and flow through the body.

For the purpose of truthfulness, lapis lazuli, a stunning stone with darker blue hues, can be employed. Acquiring lapis lazuli is not overly costly. Additionally, a blue sapphire can also be utilized.These stones will aid in speaking one's truth and prevent issues associated with gossiping or speaking negatively about others. They will also assist in maintaining honesty in interpersonal engagements and uphold one's commitments.

Chakra of the Throat: Meditation

The throat chakra is linked to energy levels in the blue part of the spectrum, so during basic meditations, envision blue lights. When meditating, wear blue and decorate the meditation space with blue items, such as pillows, rugs, and drapes. The presence of blue carpet in a room can create a soft and comforting energy.

Assume the easy pose position and consider tilting your head slightly back to open up the throat area during this meditation.Sitting on a blue cushion while doing throat chakra meditations can also be beneficial. Not only does it bring more blue light energy to the meditation, but it also helps elevate the spine a bit, thus aiding in the opening of the throat chakra.

Close your eyes and start breathing calmly.Visualize a blue ball of light against the dark space and see it slowly approaching you. As the ball of light moves through space, observe the shades of blue changing, starting from a light baby blue color, progressing through various turquoise shades, and gradually darkening to the deep blue hues of lapis lazuli stones.Then, witness it gradually becoming lighter and repeat the color sequence.

Observe the ball of light getting closer and closer until it is right in front of you, enveloping your body in gentle blue light.Inhale deeply and imagine the light energy entering your lungs, passing through the throat area, and healing the larynx. Then, envision the blue light energy filling your entire body, and as you exhale, witness the blue light gradually leaving your body.

Continue this exercise for 15-30 minutes, gradually changing the color of the light to inhale light of different energy levels. This will aid in healing all aspects of the throat chakra, from resolving insecurities about speaking your truth to enhancing your ability to listen to others and facilitate their healing.

When it comes to meditating on spiritual chakras, I have discovered that using guided meditations can be beneficial. You can find guided meditations in mobile apps or for free on YouTube. They can assist you in incorporating the appropriate colors of light, pleasant music, meditative sounds, and mantras. Aim to spend two to three weeks meditating specifically on the throat chakra, utilizing various methods and techniques.

As mentioned earlier, many aspects of the throat chakra are interconnected with the solar plexus and heart chakras. Consequently, it may be beneficial to practice balancing and healing meditations for all three chakras simultaneously. Here is my approach:

Begin by assuming the easy pose and breathe calmly and naturally. Visualize a spinning disk of yellow light approaching and let it enter your body, moving up towards the root chakra. The disk should move at a constant speed, gradually passing through the sacral chakra and coming to rest in the solar plexus. Once in the solar plexus, envision the size and brightness of the disk increasing, accompanied by bright yellow colors. Experience the pleasant and calming effects of the energy while observing the spinning disk of light. Allow it to grow as you inhale and shrink slightly as you exhale. Keep it in the solar plexus chakra for approximately five minutes, then watch it move out of the solar plexus and gradually ascend towards the heart chakra, transforming into a vibrant green color.

As it reaches the chest area, let it turn deep and bright green and remain in the heart chakra area for another five minutes.Stay focused on the light as you breathe in and out calmly and methodically. Since the heart chakra is a higher energy point, visualize the disk spinning faster.

Next, watch the disk exit the heart chakra area and begin ascending towards the throat chakra. Allow it to gradually blend blue with the green to create shades of turquoise and aquamarine. As it settles into the throat chakra area, feel its warmth enveloping and soothing your throat. Increase the speed of the spinning disk, allowing it to absorb higher frequencies of spiritual energy, and observe it taking on darker shades of blue.Meditate on the throat chakra for another five minutes or so, then slowly watch the light fade away to end your meditation. This meditation not only heals all three chakras simultaneously but also assists in properly balancing them.

Words of Wisdom for the Throat Chakra

The throat chakra, which is a spiritually oriented chakra with higher energy, can be greatly influenced by the subconscious mind and the programming you received during your youth. To reprogram the throat chakra, affirmations can be used. By consistently reciting affirmations for the throat chakra, they will progressively seep into your subconscious mind and rewire it to manifest improved behaviors. The subconscious mind is akin to a computer that lacks intelligence and requires clear instructions. Through daily affirmations, you possess the ability to control your subconscious mind.

1. I can express myself clearly and confidently.
2. I consistently speak the truth.
3. I am dependable and honor my commitments.
4. When I feel mistreated, I calmly and confidently communicate my concerns.
5. I never feel a lump in my throat when I need to speak up.
6. Speaking to others feels comfortable for me.
7. I find satisfaction in public speaking.
8. I am a self-assured speaker.
9. The words I utter always align with the truth.
10. I delight in sharing my ideas with others.
11. When I convey my thoughts through writing, I express only the truth.
12. Fearlessly, I voice my opinions without hesitation.
13. I take responsibility for speaking the truth.
14. I feel secure when honestly expressing myself to others.
15. I abstain from using communication to harm others in any manner.
16. I freely speak the truth without fear.

8

Chakra of the Third Eye

When we reach the third eye chakra, we are entering the realm of purely spiritual energy centers. While the throat chakra is connected to bridging the inner world of thoughts and ideas with the outer physical world, the third eye chakra is about establishing a connection with the greater reality that envelops us. It is through the third eye chakra that we access our intuition and psychic abilities. Many individuals struggle with this aspect because they do not believe in the psychic realm, yet it is just as real as any other experience. The key lies in being receptive and open to receiving and embracing it. By opening your third eye chakra, you will discover newfound realities previously unimaginable, fostering deeper connections with others and the spiritual world that surrounds and permeates our existence.

The Third Eye Chakra: What Is It?

The third eye chakra, positioned in the area between the eyebrows, just above the physical eyes, is believed by some to actually be located in the brain behind this spot, and it is closely associated with the pineal gland. Unlike the physical eyes, the third eye is attuned to different types of energy and allows for a form of "seeing" that extends beyond visible light in the physical realm.

Indigo is the color associated with the third eye, representing a bluish-purple shade of high energy. It is important to note that one should not attempt to open the third eye until all the lower chakras are open and balanced, and some experience with meditation has been gained.

Referred to as Ajna in Sanskrit, the third eye's element is light, reflecting its spiritual and highly energetic nature. It exists beyond the constraints of time and transcends physical reality. The third eye has the capability to enhance one's perception and enable them to see what cannot be perceived by ordinary physical senses. This includes gaining insight into the future and the past, as well as perceiving the present in unconventional ways.

Often associated with one's intuition, the third eye chakra acts as the source of gut feelings. Trusting these intuitive feelings is crucial since they often provide valuable information about people and situations, even if that information is sensed rather than easily articulated. Intuition can reveal the true nature of others, allowing for the detection of their intentions, whether they are genuine or harmful.Unfortunately, many individuals disregard their intuition due to societal conditioning.

In recent times, there has been a prevailing materialistic view of the universe, dismissing the existence of psychic powers and attributing intuition to mere illusion. This perspective overlooks the fact that physical reality is not the sole reality within this universe. The universe and its inhabitants exist on multiple dimensions, including higher vibrational frequencies and spiritual dimensions that envelop the physical universe. Failing to acknowledge and pay attention to these spiritual aspects leads to a lack of awareness. Cultures throughout history have acknowledged and tapped into the spiritual realm, but dismissing or discounting it can result in the inability to recognize intuitive experiences as meaningful.

During our earthly existence, our physical bodies limit our ability to fully experience the spiritual world. As a result, we catch glimpses of it in subtle moments and fleeting experiences. However, as one progresses spiritually, the existence of the spiritual world becomes increasingly evident and intense.

In addition to instinctive intuitions or experiencing small occurrences like knowing when a friend is about to call before they actually do, you can also receive information through dreams. Many individuals with fully awakened third eyes experience lucid dreaming. These dreams often reveal forthcoming events, but they can also contain experiences from past lives.

The initial step to opening the third eye is simply allowing yourself to have these experiences. Start by becoming more consciously aware of any psychic or intuitive occurrences you may be having. Instead of disregarding them, begin to heighten your awareness. By consciously acknowledging spiritual experiences, you will begin to develop your sense of them. It is similar to any other skill; if you neglect to exercise a specific muscle, it will gradually weaken and become useless. Likewise, our psychic and intuitive abilities, including the third eye, exist within all of us. However, they may lie inactive if we haven't utilized them.

The third eye chakra is the pathway to accessing your spiritual gifts. Some individuals mistakenly believe that certain people are naturally talented in this realm while the rest of us lack such abilities. However, this is not true. All of us possess these abilities; the key is to recognize and start utilizing them while increasing our awareness of them. There is no limit to the personal power you can tap into by using your psychic abilities.

To utilize the third eye safely, it is crucial to have an open and healed heart and throat chakra.

The third eye allows us to perceive hidden truths and provides inner guidance for navigating life more successfully. It not only connects us with concealed realities but also allows us to comprehend deeper truths and grasp realities that surpass verbal expression and logical comprehension.

If mindfulness is your goal, opening the third eye can assist you in achieving it. Opening the third eye chakra is an essential step for anyone seeking spiritual growth.

The Complete Unbroken Realm

In Western culture, there is a tendency to break down the world into distinct objects and processes. This can be seen as a mechanistic worldview. We perceive the universe and everything in it as separate and individual.

However, the true nature of the universe is dualistic. While there are individual entities within it, the belief that they are completely independent and individualistic is an illusion. Simultaneously, there exists an unbroken wholeness and totality. As an individual within the universe, you are also connected to the entirety of it, albeit in a small isolated corner.

The third eye represents the first chakra that possesses a holistic aspect. By awakening the third eye, one can enhance their ability to perceive and experience the unbroken wholeness of existence. Opening the third eye facilitates the connection with inner wisdom as well as the spiritual wisdom present in the Higher Self and Universal Consciousness.

Some individuals may progress quickly in their spiritual growth and may find themselves capable of astral travel in addition to lucid dreaming. However, it is important not to be discouraged if these abilities do not immediately manifest. Each person's spiritual development unfolds uniquely and at their own pace. It is possible to engage in astral travel during the dream state without conscious awareness of it, and such experiences are often disregarded as mere dreams. Changing one's perspective can lead to a different understanding of the world.

The third eye chakra can also enable communication with spirit guides. In essence, the third eye acts as a gateway to the spiritual and divine realms. It allows one to access information and knowledge through sources other than the five physical senses.

Knowledge and Morality

The third eye is the source of wisdom as well. By opening the third eye, you can harmonize the creativity from the sacral chakra, the self-assurance and leadership qualities from the solar plexus chakra, and the expressive abilities from the throat chakra. However, it is important to remember that not all ideas are good ideas.Nonetheless, by developing and activating the third eye chakra, you can infuse wisdom into the creative energies of the sacral chakra and steer your ideas towards benefiting humanity and all living beings. Opening the third eye also promotes a sense of balance, tolerance, and open-mindedness.It grants a strong connection to both inner wisdom and the collective wisdom of the Universal Consciousness, which are both advantageous outcomes of awakening the third eye.

Different individuals will have varying degrees of psychic awareness and may tune in to different aspects of it. For some, lucid dreaming may be more pronounced than others. Some may become clairvoyant, possessing the ability to receive clear visions. These visions may be glimpses into the future or provide knowledge about events and information that normal means cannot access. Others may develop clairaudience, where information is transmitted through sounds or voices. Claircognizance, on the other hand, involves suddenly "knowing" something.These gifts exist in varying degrees in all of us, so they are not mutually exclusive. It is unnecessary to worry about having one gift over the others or getting caught up in their specific definitions. Instead, embrace an open mindset and allow the experiences to unfold naturally over time.

Moreover, the third eye is closely tied to your life's direction and your sense of purpose. Typically, this is experienced as a higher sense of purpose that goes beyond mere career or material aspirations. It may also manifest as a communal, spiritual, and ethical purpose that transcends individualism.

How Does a Blocked Third Eye Chakra Occur?

When your experiences are dismissed or ridiculed, it can lead to the blocking of the third eye. This can happen when we share spiritual or psychic encounters and are met with mockery.Such discounting of our experiences, especially during childhood, can have a significant impact on the third eye, causing it to become blocked.

The larger society we live in also contributes to the blockage of the third eye. Society as a whole embraces a materialistic outlook, dismissing anything beyond the physical world and considering science as the only valid source of knowledge.Psychic experiences are disregarded, and intuition is considered mere wishful thinking or mere coincidences.Belief in spirituality is often seen as outdated, and any spiritual encounters are deemed illusions, products of an overly active mind, or even signs of mental illness.

Even though we may be unaware of it, these prevalent attitudes in our surroundings continually influence and shape our subconscious, making it more challenging for us to open our third eye and doubt any psychic or intuitive encounters we may have. Without realizing it, we might even adopt a skeptical mindset rooted in materialism and scientism, which hinders us from fully experiencing the richness of the world that surrounds us.

Traumatic experiences can also contribute to the blocking of the third eye. Any experience that results in post-traumatic stress disorder or the lasting effects of childhood abuse can effectively block the third eye.

Signs of a Blockage in the Third Eye Chakra

We all possess an inner voice, and the initial indication of an obstruction in the third eye is the tendency to disregard or neglect this inner voice.Some individuals may even reach a point where their inner voice is silenced. Once this occurs, they become desensitized to the information revealed to them through their sixth sense.

One symptom of a blocked third eye is fear of the future.This arises due to the interconnectedness of time, with the past, present, and future forming a continuous fabric. This connection holds a psychic nature and severing it results in an overwhelming sense of uncertainty, which subsequently leads to fear of the future. Anxiety can often arise as a consequence.

If you are experiencing anxiety, it is important to closely examine it in order to determine its origins. Keep in mind that anxiety can develop when the root chakra is blocked. To distinguish between this type of anxiety and anxiety stemming from a third eye blockage, consider the focus of the anxiety. If it pertains to one's basic safety and security, it is closely related to the root chakra. Conversely, if the anxiety is primarily future-oriented, it may be a result of a third eye blockage. Often, both chakras can be blocked simultaneously, as it is impossible to have fully balanced higher chakras when the root chakra is obstructed. If anxiety persists, it is advisable to engage in root chakra meditations first and then proceed to meditate on the third eye chakra.

Excessive skepticism is a prominent symptom of a blocked third eye. Individuals with a blockage tend to rationalize it by emphasizing logic and displaying an overwhelming degree of skepticism. You may have encountered people who question everything, constantly demanding proof for any event or phenomenon. These individuals are overly engrossed in the scientific way of thinking. While science is a valuable tool with numerous applications in our society, problems arise when it takes on a quasi-religious role, rather than being viewed as the tool that it is. Unfortunately, the tendency to view science through religious lenses is becoming increasingly prevalent, leading to more people experiencing obstructions in their third eye and crown chakras. This shift in attitude towards scientism is gradually permeating and merging with our materialistic consumerist lifestyle.

This takes us to another point that demonstrates the indications of a blocked third eye chakra. When the third eye is blocked, some individuals become excessively focused on material possessions. By blocking the third eye, you are essentially obstructing an essential aspect of your identity. A person is much more than just a physical entity; they are a complete and integrated entity comprised of the physical, mental, emotional, and spiritual aspects. When both the third eye and crown chakras are blocked, we are severing the spiritual essence that makes us whole and complete.

This creates a void that exists within our lives. This void needs to be filled in some way, so people attempt to fill it through meaningless materialism. One approach is by filling their lives with material goods, believing that purchasing extravagant clothing, jewelry, and electronic gadgets will fulfill their inner needs and provide a sense of completeness.Another method is through the pursuit of endless entertainment. Our society readily supplies mindless entertainment through endless television programs, sporting events, video games, and pornography. Of course, it is healthy and beneficial to engage in some of these activities as part of a balanced lifestyle. However, many people try to occupy every moment of their existence with some form of entertainment because their third eye chakra is blocked and they are disconnecting completely from their spiritual and psychic existence.

One issue with this is that these attempts to replace the spiritual with material and entertainment are never effective. This leaves individuals feeling as if their lives are devoid of meaning and can even lead to an existential crisis in some cases.Some individuals may attempt to fill this void with drugs and alcohol, leading to a blocked sacral chakra in addition to the blocked third eye chakra.

In summary, the symptoms of a blocked third eye chakra include an increased or excessive skepticism, a feeling and belief that the material world is the only reality, a sense of life being meaningless, and a vague but prevalent feeling that one's own life lacks purpose. Regardless of having a career and a healthy solar plexus chakra, if your third eye is blocked, you may struggle to find a sense of purpose and meaning associated with your life and work. Depression is a common symptom of a blocked third eye chakra, and as previously discussed, anxiety about the future can also indicate a blocked or healing-needing third eye chakra.

The third eye can also become overactive. Reinforcing the normal and healthy functioning of the third eye chakra can help us understand the consequences when the third eye is overactive. Excessive and intrusive psychic information may occur. This floodgate of information can result in delusions, as your mind becomes saturated with information that may not be relevant or even real.An overactive third eye may cause auditory and visual hallucinations, as an overwhelming amount of information floods in and overwhelms your senses, potentially leading you to occupy a state of meaninglessness that resides between the psychic and physical realms.

The excessive information that is affecting your senses may also affect your mind.When this occurs, it can result in paranoid thinking patterns. This phenomenon happens when intuitive information becomes overwhelming and is perceived by the mind rather than the physical senses. Often, this information is misinterpreted because individuals experiencing these situations are not necessarily aware of the third eye and genuine intuition.

Another indication of a blockage in the third eye is an excessive ego-based mindset. This is because when the third eye is open, one becomes connected with the universe and Universal Consciousness, causing the ego to have a diminished role in perceptions. In contrast, when the third eye is blocked, excessive energy can concentrate in the root, sacral, and solar plexus chakras. This leads to a heightened focus on the self and one's own needs, while diminishing the connection with the rest of the universe.

When the third eye is blocked, one is unable to accurately perceive the entirety of reality. This can leave individuals feeling cynical and disconnected, with a tendency to blame others or external circumstances for their life situation.Blocking the third eye also cuts off access to a great deal of wisdom and spiritual connection that extends beyond the self.

The ability to visualize is limited when the third eye is blocked. The third eye is not solely involved in psychic phenomena but also in the type of visualization that sparks invention, creates great artwork, and enables the imagination necessary for writing a play, developing a movie, or starting a business. An open third eye enhances imagination and opens up new possibilities. Conversely, a blocked third eye leads to a lack of imagination and feeling trapped in the present moment. Many influential figures in society such as Da Vinci, Mozart, and Steve Jobs tapped into the power of the third eye to ignite their creativity. Creative individuals not only have an open sacral chakra but also an open third eye.Many creative insights arise from a connection with the Universal Consciousness. Creatives often express that their insights seem to appear without conscious effort.

A blocked third eye can restrict creative abilities by severing this connection. Those who merely get by in life, solely working to meet survival needs and perhaps dreaming of retirement and comfort, often have a blocked third eye chakra.

When the third eye is blocked, visualizing something in the future becomes a limited or eliminated capacity of the human spirit. This explains how the world's leading creative individuals can truly change the world. Through their open third eye, they can perceive not only the world as it is, but also envision multiple possibilities for the future. Historical figures like Thomas Edison were able to utilize the third eye, consciously or unconsciously, to see things that did not yet exist and imagine how they could transform society and people's lives in new and different ways.

Individuals with a blocked third eye also suffer from indecisiveness, particularly when making choices about their future path in life. Indecision can plague them, leading to a lack of action or dissatisfaction with the choices they do make.

Surprisingly, a lack of common sense is also a manifestation of a blocked third eye chakra. This is evident in today's culture, where the pursuit of "education" is elevated while everyday common sense is underappreciated. It is important to recognize the value of education, but not at the expense of common sense and intuition, which are two vital gifts.

Fears

This symptom is particularly noteworthy. If your third eye becomes overactive or obstructed, you may have very vivid and unpleasant nightmares or dreams. These nightmares frequently involve a spiritual element that seems to be an evil force. These nightmares could cause you to feel uneasy and intimidated when you wake up. Should these kinds of nightmares start to occur frequently, it's a clear indication that you are experiencing issues with the third eye chakra. To help focus the right energy, immediate attention should be given to affirmations, meditation, and the use of crystals.

The Gland of Pineal

Some individuals believe that the third eye originates from the pineal gland, a small organ closely linked to the brain. Although many in the medical community claim that the pineal gland serves no practical purpose, it actually functions as a relay station for receiving and transmitting psychic energy. Calcification of the pineal gland can occur, and one of the main contributors to this process is the consumption of fluoridated water. Eliminating the use of fluoridated water can greatly contribute to healing and decalcifying the pineal gland, which may be sufficient to awaken the third eye for some individuals. There are numerous supplements and tonics available to detoxify and decalcify the pineal gland.

The pineal gland is closely associated with our sleep-wake cycle, and when it becomes calcified, our sleep-wake cycle may be adversely affected. Our circadian rhythm may not align properly with the natural daylight cycle our bodies are designed for, resulting in a tendency to be awake at night ("night owl") and difficulties in obtaining a full night's sleep, necessitating frequent naps.

Excessive intake of calcium can lead to calcification of the pineal gland. To ensure appropriate calcium levels, it is advisable to avoid calcium supplements and obtain calcium from natural sources instead. Various natural sources of calcium, such as whole milk, cheese, and leafy green vegetables like spinach, can help maintain adequate calcium levels. Synthetic calcium should be avoided if possible.

While many people express concerns about fluoridated toothpaste, the main concern lies in the consumption of fluoridated water. If fluoridated water intake is eliminated, toothpaste should not pose a significant issue. Simply avoid swallowing toothpaste, and the minimal and inconsequential amount of fluoride exposure that may occur in such cases can be mitigated.

There are several supplements available for decalcifying the pineal gland. Iodine is a primary substance people turn to for this purpose, which can be taken in the form of iodine supplements or drops. Additionally, increasing iodine intake can be achieved by incorporating sea kelp into your diet, such as adding dried seaweed to soups, broths, and meals.

Turmeric is believed to aid in decalcifying the pineal gland by counteracting the toxic effects of excessive fluoride in the body.If the use of fluoridated toothpaste continues, taking a turmeric supplement can help maintain a healthy balance.

A supplement called Activator X is also considered beneficial for the pineal gland. Activator X contains vitamins K1 and K2, which are vital for overall health as well as supporting the pineal gland.

Signs of a Blocked Third Eye Chakra in the Body

Physical symptoms may arise when the third eye chakra is blocked. It is important to pay attention to these symptoms, especially if they coincide with mental and emotional signs of a blocked third eye chakra.Chronic headaches, including migraines, could indicate a blockage in the third eye chakra. Insomnia, particularly when accompanied by intense nightmares, is also a significant symptom of a blocked third eye.Discomfort in the eyes, front of the skull, or temple region may be a result of a blockage in the third eye chakra.Visual disturbances or a sudden deterioration in visual quality may also occur. Individuals who wear contact lenses might notice that their lenses no longer function properly. Dryness, pain, and irritation in the eyes may be experienced as well. A scratchy sensation may develop when the third eye chakra is blocked.

Awakening of the Third Eye

If you begin to practice meditation on the third eye, don't be alarmed if you experience unusual symptoms. It is possible that you may feel pressure in the center of your brow, which is a natural sensation indicating energy flowing through the third eye as it opens.Additionally, ringing in the ears and other uncommon symptoms may occur as the third eye fully awakens, potentially for the first time since childhood. It is also possible to have vivid dreams upon awakening. However, there is no cause for concern unless these dreams are negative. In that case, using third eye meditation can help resolve the issue. Once your third eye is awakened, you will experience lucid dreaming, but the dreams themselves will not be frightening. Instead, they will serve as a means of communication, conveying information and enlightenment. These dreams can be so vivid that they feel indistinguishable from reality, as they hold a certain degree of reality within them.Therefore, it is advisable to prepare yourself for this possibility through meditation and other techniques.

To ensure a positive experience during the awakening of the third eye, it is beneficial to heal the heart and throat chakras. The nature of your experiences during the spiritual journey of the chakras will largely depend on your level of spiritual development and growth thus far. If you are unprepared, you may find it challenging to cope with the energies being unleashed, which can lead to nightmares, disturbing visions, and other difficulties. Therefore, if you find yourself experiencing negative effects, such as bad dreams, it is recommended to step back and focus on healing the heart chakra first, followed by the throat chakra.

Consider the consequences of opening up spiritual and psychic energies while being engulfed in negativity, potentially lacking love, acceptance, empathy, and truth. This is why it is crucial to work on the lower chakras before attempting to awaken the third eye. All of the chakras play a role in this process. For instance, a healthy root chakra is essential for a sense of safety and security overall. Similarly, a well-functioning solar plexus chakra is necessary for self-confidence and self-assurance, both of which are vital for accepting and managing powerful, intuitive, and psychic energies.

It is crucial to acknowledge the existence of evil both in the world and the universe.This is why it can be problematic to awaken the third eye without a solid foundation. Please do not misunderstand this statement. We are not implying that you are a bad person. However, it is important to be aware that these negative energies are present and can become active when a person is not adequately prepared.

This underscores the significance of focusing on the heart chakra. Love and understanding have the power to neutralize evil energies. By fully healing and opening the heart chakra, you can increase the love energy within your spirit. Achieving higher levels of development necessitates reaching the point where you genuinely feel and experience unconditional love, empathy, and forgiveness for all individuals.

Once this is accomplished, it is crucial to ensure that the throat chakra is completely opened and healed. Remember our discussion about the throat chakra and how we emphasized the consequences of gossiping or using speech for dishonest or malicious purposes, as well as the importance of honoring your word. These may seem like fundamental values, but they are also integral to spiritual coherence. The essence of goodness lies in truth. In contrast, evil thrives on deceit and falsehood. When you understand this perspective, you can comprehend the importance of healing the throat chakra alongside the heart chakra before embarking on a third eye awakening and connecting with spiritual dimensions beyond our physical universe.

Foods for Chakra of the Third Eye

When focusing on healing and opening the third eye chakra, it is beneficial to incorporate dark-colored and purple foods into your diet. Grapes (red, purple, and black), blackberries, and blueberries are excellent food choices for this purpose. Additionally, including eggplant, purple carrots, and purple potatoes in your meals can also support the third eye chakra.

Practicing mindful eating is significant for the third eye chakra. As we delve into the spiritual realm with this chakra, our intention and purpose while eating can impact the opening of the third eye. Trusting your intuition is crucial as well. Sometimes, the third eye communicates through subtle signs that we may not fully recognize. By paying closer attention to even the slightest intuitive impulses, you can enhance your intuitive abilities. Intuition often surfaces when making food choices. If you notice your intuition guiding you towards a particular food, it is best to follow it rather than overthink or doubt it.Consume the foods that your third eye is directing you to consume.

Furthermore, there are other foods that can support the third eye, specifically those rich in omega-three fatty acids.Incorporating bluefish, salmon, and mackerel into your diet can be beneficial. Walnuts are also beneficial for the third eye, and the omega-three fatty acids they contain play a practical role in protecting brain health, which in turn enhances the third eye and the pineal gland.

Essential Oils for Chakra of the Third Eye

For the third eye and crown chakras, aromatherapy and essential oils are more significant than for the lower chakras. Seek for potent holy oils such as myrrh and frankincense. Made from a purple flower, Clary is similarly beneficial for the chakra located just above the third eye. Juniper is beneficial as well. For balance and to assist in opening the third eye, use aromatherapy.

Chakra's Colors for the Third Eye

The color indigo, which is bluish-purple in hue, is linked to the third eye chakra. When repairing the third eye, you can combine purple and dark blue colors. Owing to the chakra's spiritual significance, I choose to utilize candles in my work on opening it. Use blue or purple candles together, if you can find them. The third eye energy can be unlocked by lighting the candles whenever you want and inhaling the scents. Using purple candles during meditation periods can also be beneficial. You can also wear purple apparel and embellish your meditation area with items in dark blue and purple hues.

Crystals for the Chakra of the Third Eye

The third eye chakra is often associated with the beloved amethyst crystal, which commonly exhibits various hues such as purple, white, and occasionally, flecks of gold. This potent crystal possesses the ability to harness spiritual energies, making it ideal for meditation or as a talisman for unblocking the third eye. Another suitable option for the third eye is lapis lazuli, a deep blue stone that has the capacity to channel energies not only for the third eye but also for the throat chakra. Due to its alignment with the higher vibrational states of the throat chakra, lapis lazuli is considered more spiritually inclined.Utilizing this stone can be advantageous in maintaining an open and healed throat chakra, an essential aspect of awakening the third eye.

Chakra of the Third Eye: Meditation

When practicing meditation for the third eye, it is recommended to direct the energy towards the middle of the forehead. As always, you can choose to meditate in a comfortable position with your eyes closed, and focus on regular breathing. At the beginning of your meditation, concentrate on the location of the third eye. While breathing, consciously observe any feelings of pressure, warmth, or energy in the center of the forehead. As you do this, visualize a sphere of purple light approaching you. Envision it as dark surroundings with intensely vibrant and fluorescent purple colors. Allow the light to approach you and visualize it emitting a beam of energy. Let this beam of energy connect with the center of your forehead, where the third eye chakra is located. Now, visualize the light traveling all the way through your head and exiting at the back of your head. The third eye is often perceived as extending throughout the brain and toward the back of the head. Therefore, it is beneficial to visualize the beam of light going all the way through.Maintain this meditation for 15 minutes, and then visualize the beam of light shutting off gradually, causing the energy sphere to disappear before your eyes. You may feel tired and breathe heavily after this experience, so focus on your breath and return to a state of calmness as you conclude your meditation practice.

Some individuals find that they can enhance the flow of energy into the third eye by placing their hands together in a prayer position during their meditation sessions. You can also try this technique whenever you need a quick healing or meditation session throughout the day. Simply close your eyes, bring your hands into a prayer position, and allow the energy to pass through the forehead area while concentrating on that specific area and being fully aware of all the sensations you are feeling.

Recitations for the Chakra of the Third Eye

- We'll go over a few affirmations that work well with the third eye chakra in this part.
- I am deserving of getting intuitive information and I am trusting.
- My intuition is reliable.
- I'll pay attention to my intuition.
- I am receptive to creative thought and imagery.
- I'll learn whatever the universe has to teach me.
- I will pay attention to and trust my feelings.
- I look within for insight and direction.
- I have faith in the universal consciousness' light.
- I'm receptive and welcoming.
- I have intuition.
- Higher Truths are acceptable to me.
- I trusted my intuition to lead me to the truth.
- Eternal potential is the domain of spiritual truth.

9

The Crown Chakra

The crown chakra, which is the most spiritual and highest among all the chakras, will be thoroughly examined in this chapter. It will focus on the role it plays in one's life and provide insights on how to open and heal it. However, it is crucial to ensure that the other chakras are already healed and balanced before attempting to heal the crown chakra. This entails healing the root, sacral, solar plexus, heart, throat, and third eye chakras prior to opening the crown chakra.

Opening the crown chakra is vital for spiritual growth, but it requires patience. It is ill-advised to try opening the crown chakra until all the other chakras have been successfully opened and one has experienced the spiritual journey associated with each chakra individually.

Once the crown chakra is opened, one can enhance their spirituality by pursuing a complete third eye awakening and kundalini awakening.However, it is important to remain patient and allow growth to occur naturally over time. This spiritual awakening will follow its own appropriate course according to the natural order of things.

The Crown Chakra: What Is It?

The crown chakra symbolizes our highest level of spirituality and the link between our spiritual self and the Universal Consciousness. Additionally, it represents our connection to our own Higher Self, serving as a connection between our physical and mental bodies and our spiritual body or Higher Self. Furthermore, it is linked to the duality of our universe, allowing us to connect our individuality to the Universal Consciousness.

Although some argue that the crown chakra exists slightly outside the body and above the crown of the head, its exact physical location is not essential for your studies, spiritual growth, or meditations.

The colors associated with the crown chakra hold great spiritual significance, with purple being its main color. Purple reflects the higher vibrational state of this highly energetic chakra, as it represents the highest energy state visible light can assume. Consequently, purple is strongly associated with the crown chakra.

The crown chakra is also associated with the color white, symbolizing the unity of all the other chakras. White, being a combination of all the colors of the rainbow, represents the amalgamation and balance of the root, sacral, solar plexus, heart, throat, third eye, and crown chakras. The presence of abundant white light in your life signifies a greater sense of balance.

Moreover, the crown chakra embodies the color gold, which when blended with purple and white, represents royalty and divinity. These colors can be combined and found in a single crystal.

In Sanskrit, the crown chakra is referred to as Sahasrara, also known as Niralambapuri and Shunnya. Visualize the crown chakra as a thousand-petaled purple lotus flower. This chakra does not have an associated element as it represents the connection with the divine and cannot be tied to any physical element.However, if it were to be associated with one, it could be likened to the Higgs Boson field, which permeates the entire universe, providing energy and meaning to everything.

Harnessing the power of the crown chakra is the ultimate achievement in spiritual growth before reaching more advanced states, such as a kundalini awakening. The crown chakra can be linked to the pituitary gland, serving as the connection between our physical bodies and the reality that transcends our imagination.

Energetically, envision your body forming a loop where energy can flow from the top of your head to the base of your spine, forming a connection between the crown chakra and the root chakra. This energy flow occurs as you open each of the chakras during meditation.

Beyond its relationship to the physical body, the crown chakra is closely connected to the brain and nervous system. However, its significance extends far beyond the physical realm. The crown chakra serves as a connection point between your mind, body, soul, and the spiritual realms of existence.

Many individuals desire to understand how they can incorporate the chakras into their daily lives, including the crown chakra. Fortunately, yogi practitioners and gurus possess a comprehensive understanding of the crown chakra, enabling anyone to unlock its potential and utilize its power. The crown chakra is primarily associated with the brain and consciousness, as the brain alone would be insignificant without its connection to the crown chakra and the spiritual realm beyond. Through this connection, consciousness is brought to life.

However, the crown chakra offers more than just consciousness; it also serves as a gateway to connect our physical existence with a deeper spiritual realm. While the third eye chakra contributes to this connection to some extent, it is through the crown chakra that we establish a bond with the divine. It is essential to recognize that the universe possesses a dual nature - one aspect characterized by physicality with individual beings and objects, and another aspect as a unified and unbroken whole. The crown chakra acts as the bridge between these two dimensions of existence, allowing us to connect with the formless and timeless essence of all that is. Through the crown chakra, we can establish a link with the Universal Consciousness that surrounds us and is an integral part of our own conscious being.

Moreover, the crown chakra enables us to connect with spirit guides and departed souls that have influenced our lives. It provides an avenue for reuniting with loved ones from our past, including family members, friends, and even beloved pets. Additionally, through the crown chakra, we can establish a connection with Spirit Guides who possess infinite wisdom beyond the physical realm. This spiritual connection facilitates the attainment of higher states of being that are otherwise unattainable.

Individuals who have opened their crown chakra often experience a profound connection and love for all living beings. This state of pure bliss transcends judgment and other characteristics that are prevalent in the ordinary physical world, which is driven by ego and competition. It reveals an unbroken whole that represents the Divine, with us being an integral part of it. Acknowledging the duality of the Universe, we understand that as individuals existing within this Divine whole, we must undergo a learning phase to evolve and become a harmonious part of it.

Opening the crown chakra serves as a gateway to accessing our Higher Self, enabling us to reach a state of peace, harmony, and bliss.

How Does a Blocked Crown Chakra Occur?

Blockages of lower chakras can obstruct the crown chakra, which may be surprising due to its lower position. A blockage of the heart chakra, in particular, can affect the crown chakra. This is because the heart chakra is closely linked to our connection with other living beings. While the heart chakra pertains to our earthly connections, any connection with a conscious being is associated with spirituality. Failing to establish a basic connection with other physical beings hampers the formation of spiritual connections with the larger spiritual realm.

Consequently, shallow or dysfunctional relationships in the physical world can lead to a blockage of the crown chakra. Moreover, an excessively developed or hyperactive ego can also result in a blockage. While it is important to focus on cultivating a healthy solar plexus chakra during the development of lower chakras, overemphasizing this chakra can unbalance the crown chakra. The solar plexus chakra is connected to the development and elevation of the self or ego, which can become excessive if taken to extremes. On the other hand, the crown chakra emphasizes the unity of the self with the Universal Consciousness. It is crucial to understand that this unity does not involve erasing the self, but rather, merging one's consciousness with the vast and encompassing universal consciousness. In other words, it involves retaining one's individuality while simultaneously joining consciousness with the unified whole that represents the universe.

Signs of a Blockage in the Crown Chakra

A blocked crown chakra can appear as a cynical attitude towards spirituality and the belief in a nonphysical aspect of existence, similar to the third eye. The crown chakra is associated with connectivity to both conscious beings and the Universal Consciousness, so feeling disconnected from others is a common symptom of blockage. Closed-mindedness and skepticism are often displayed by individuals with a blocked crown chakra, as they demand physical proof for things. Conversely, some individuals may have an overactive crown chakra, causing them to feel disconnected from their bodies. It is important to maintain balance and recognize the importance of the physical body while exploring the chakras. When the crown chakra is blocked, one tends to disbelieve in any existence beyond the physical world, displaying skepticism and not acknowledging any form of existence beyond the present. People with blocked crown chakras may doubt the existence of conscious minds and question whether other living beings, such as animals, possess self-consciousness or a life that extends beyond the physical body. A sense of purpose is often missing in the lives of those with blocked crown chakras, which can create an existential sense within them. Despite its spiritual nature, a blocked crown chakra can hinder the ability to connect with others, resulting in feelings of isolation, loneliness, and disconnection from family members and spirituality. Some individuals may even feel anger towards God and blame Him for their lack of success or dissatisfaction with their life circumstances.

A blocked crown chakra can cause an inability to set and achieve goals, although it can be difficult to differentiate this from other chakra blockages that produce similar symptoms, such as a blocked solar plexus chakra. The goals affected by a blocked solar plexus chakra are usually more physical, ego-driven, and straightforward, while a blocked crown chakra may hinder one's ability to reach lofty or spiritual goals. If uncertain, working on all the chakras can help determine the cause.

However, a lack of direction in general is always associated with a blocked crown chakra. A healthy and open crown chakra is linked to individuals who can set and achieve goals, and have a clear sense of direction.

An overactive crown chakra can result in an excessive attachment to the spiritual side of life. Although it is true that we are spiritual beings and will eventually experience our existence through a spiritual body, our current existence is also dependent on physical lessons. Being overly fixated on the spiritual is not a sign of growth, but rather a failure to develop as required. If we are on Earth, it is because we need to learn from the physical aspects of life. Obsessively focusing on spiritual matters indicates an imbalance in the crown chakra and a lack of proper spiritual growth.

The physical symptoms of a blocked crown chakra primarily affect the nervous system. Migraine headaches are the most common symptom, along with blurred vision.Other symptoms include dizziness, blackouts, seizures, and in severe cases that last for an extended period, it can lead to neurological disorders like ALS, Parkinson's disease, and Alzheimer's. Blindness, hearing loss, and stroke can also occur.

Foods for the Chakra of the Crown

When considering foods that benefit the crown chakra, it is important to have a broad perspective. Incorporating white-colored foods such as white or yellow carrots and white cauliflower into your diet can aid in the healing of the crown chakra. Additionally, including purple foods like eggplant, blueberries, and purple potatoes, which we have previously discussed in relation to other chakras, can be beneficial. For the crown chakra, it is advantageous to create meals that combine the colors purple, white, and gold. To unblock the crown chakra, you can mix together blueberries or blackberries for the color purple, white potatoes or cauliflower for white, and corn and butter for gold, thus creating a complete meal. Other yellow or golden foods like yellow squash, carrots, parsnip, almond, walnut, and sesame seeds can also be beneficial for the crown chakra.

Aromatherapy for the Crown Chakra

When it comes to the crown chakra, the most effective essential oils to use are those with spiritual or sacred properties. Including frankincense in your healing routine is highly recommended as it aids in achieving a state of deep meditation, spiritual connection, and receptiveness. Vetiver is another beneficial essential oil that can be used in aromatherapy or combined with other oils to promote the healing of the crown chakra. It also has the added advantage of enhancing dream clarity and recall, which plays a crucial role in fostering spiritual awareness. This oil also facilitates grounding and relaxation, making it beneficial for opening the crown chakra. If you wish to enhance the vibrational frequency, helichrysum, also known as everlasting oil, can be incorporated. This lesser-known essential oil possesses energies of a higher vibrational frequency, making it more spiritually inclined. By utilizing this high-frequency oil, you can tap into the power of your crown chakra.

The Crown Chakra's colors

Deep purple serves as the crown chakra's primary color. As the amalgamation of every hue in the rainbow, pure white holds significant importance in relation to the head chakra. Since gold is elevated as a spiritual notion, it is also linked to the crown chakra. When attempting to heal the crown chakra, you can wear all of them at once.

Crystals for the Chakra of the Crown

A variety of crystals can be used to open and repair the crown chakra. Healing the crown chakra can be greatly aided by purple amethyst, which is also used with the third eye chakra. This stone can store, receive, and transfer enormous amounts of energy. It vibrates at a high frequency. White-colored stones, such as simple and transparent quartz, are also beneficial. Pure gold is also useful for working with the crown chakra, if you have access to it.

Crown Chakra Meditation

My preferred method of crown chakra meditation is a whole balanced meditation. Follow the normal meditation protocol, but imagine a disc of light passing through each of the main chakras, rising through your body and becoming more energetic as it spins faster. Have it shift color as necessary as it moves through the seven main chakras: red, orange, yellow, green, blue, indigo, and purple. Imagine it as a white light that is flashing upward into heaven as it leaves your body at the top of your head, tying you into the Universal Consciousness.

Words of Wisdom for the Sacral Chakra

- I am finished.
- I am a spirit creature.
- It is a loving and kind universe.
- I am a part of everything and the universe.
- My guides are here to guide me.
- I am a being of light.
- I accept myself as I am; I am perfect just the way I am.
- The universe is love itself, and I am loved.

10

In summary

We appreciate your perseverance in finishing Charkas for Beginners. We hope it was educational and able to give you all the resources you require to accomplish your objectives, whatever they may be.

www.ingramcontent.com/pod-product-compliance
Lightning Source LLC
LaVergne TN
LVHW020426080526
838202LV00055B/5052